A Wildly Successful 200-Mile Hike

Lessons Learned from the Appalachian Trail

Rick Allnutt
MD, MPH, MSEE

Walk Well!
Rick Allnutt

Wayah Press
Beavercreek, Ohio

Wayah Press

© 2005 by Richard Allnutt

Printed in the United States of America. All rights reserved. No part of this work may be transcribed, transmitted, distributed, or shared in any form by and means, electronic or mechanical, including photocopying and recording systems, information storage-and-retrieval systems—except by a reviewer who may quote brief passages in a review to be printed in a magazine, newspaper, or on the Web—without written permission from the publisher.

Although the author and publisher have made every effort to ensure the accuracy and completeness of information contained in this book, We assume no responsibility for errors, inaccuracies, omissions, or any inconsistency herein. Any slights of people, places, or organizations are unintentional.

ISBN 0-9767227-0-4   978-0-9767227-0-0

LCCN 2005924167

>Cover photo is by the author of himself near Cold Mountain, Virginia

Questions regarding the content or ordering of this book should be addressed to:

>Wayah Press
>2566 Lantz Road
>Beavercreek, OH 45434
>http://www.wayahpress.com

>Orders can be sent to
>orders@imrisk.com

To my wife, Diane (EllieD) for her patience and love, to my children for their encouragement, and to the many friends I have met on the trail and in Internet hiking circles.

To my parents, Richard and Besse-Lee, who took the time to show me the outdoors as a wonderland.

Special thanks to Pam, a dear friend of the family, and to members of the Kampfire group who helped me edit this material—and especially Shane, Coy, Jack, Ralph, Helen, Tracy and Jim.

Contents

The Who, What, Where, and Whys	1
Blisters and Chafing	11
Blisters	11
Chafing	30
Knees – It's All About Prevention and Preparation	43
Losing the Will to Hike	65
The One Best Idea	101
The End of the Beginning	113
Index	117

Chapter 1

The Who, What, Where, and Whys

Sitting at Standing Indian: The mountain loomed over my shoulders as I reached the Deep Gap trailhead on a section hike of the Appalachian Trail in March of 2004. This was the middle of the Appalachian Trail (AT) thru-hiker migration and the first fellow I ran across was sitting on a log, looking up the hill.

"Hi!" I chirped as I walked up to begin my normal banter with a "thru." However this was not going to be a happy conversation. A "twenty-something," HeadsUp looked at me with hollow eyes–wistful eyes.

"How's the hike coming along?" I supported.

"Knees are wrecked.... I don't know how much further I can go," he complained in a hopeless monotone. "How far to the road on that blue blaze trail?"

I had just walked across the Kimsey Creek Trail, a blue-blazed connector to the AT from the Forest Service's Standing Indian Campground. It was a little more than four miles to the parking lot and then a couple more miles to the Rainbow Springs Campground beyond that.

It was an hour until sunset.

2 A Wildly Successful 200-Mile Hike

"I guess I'll go on up to the shelter and decide what to do in the morning," my new acquaintance said as I began the half-mile uphill segment to the Standing Indian Shelter.

He got there about dark.

We talked a little that evening. He had prepared to be on the trail for the next four months–fulfilling a dream several years old. Here we were less than 100 miles into his 2100-mile hike, and he was done. He had been excited about this trip for months, but he was about to go back home. He had to. His knees were wrecked.

So What's the Book About?

This book is about long distance hiking. My experience and most of the examples are from the Appalachian Trail (AT). The book details the three biggest problems facing a 200-mile hiker and also goes into the advantages of near-ultralight hiking.

The three problems have plagued most of the people I have seen drop off the AT either as thru-hikers or as section hikers.

The big three hike enders are:

Blisters and Chafing
Knee Pain
Losing The Will to Hike

The Who, What, Where, and Whys 3

The chapter describing ultra-light hiking is: **The one best idea–A 15-pound pack.**

The book is produced in a format and style that make it easy to carry it while hiking. There's also enough room in the margins to scribble notes and ideas.

Who Wrote It? This book is the story of how I have learned from my own mistakes (and those of others) as I have prepared to hike long distances. It offers no formula or system guaranteed to work for everyone–just one that works for me. It describes my discoveries, my failures, my ideas, and what I have tried. I am writing it in the hope that it will be of interest to a reader, but I am the first to advise hikers to work out personal answers for themselves.

My goal is to hike the Appalachian Trail–the whole thing. This is 2100+ miles along the rough, serpentine, backbone of the East Coast mountains of the United States. However, at this point in my journey, I think it is worthwhile to write about what I have learned so far.

This book is about making a good beginning. It is about the details of that experience.

After a year of preparation, I successfully hiked a continuous 200-mile section hike along the AT for my 51st birthday. I began at Springer Mountain,

4 A Wildly Successful 200-Mile Hike

Georgia on a mid-May day, and finished the long section hike 13 days later on the top of Clingman's Dome in the middle of the Smoky Mountains.

Worthwillity: As I think back on the people I have seen drop off the AT in those first two weeks of their hikes–I feel compassion and a great sense of waste.

All who walk the trail learn something about themselves. This is true whether they walk 13 miles, 200 miles, or 2100 miles. Learning is good. But I feel for everyone I meet who has dropped off the trail. I experience some of their pain as I think about all the plans and dreams and money spent on their long distance hike, gone down the drain.

My reasons for writing the book involve the dilemma that Head'sUp (with the knee pain) was facing at Deep Gap. Another part of my reasoning involves the pain I saw in good guys with rubbed-raw blisters. Blisters like these drive people off the trail at Winding Stair Gap every year. Likewise, I have seen people hobbling into Dick's Gap searching for help with chaffed thighs. What's more, I have experienced my own pains in all these anatomic areas and more. I have heard stories of nightmares that drove people from the trail. I've seen failed equipment drive people nearly mad with cold and known the problems of cold myself.

Each and every problem has a specific prevention and treatment. Learning the lessons is as important to the hiker as learning to suck is to a baby. But the schooling a hiker has to accomplish is not as instinctive as anything a baby learns. For these assignments, I have needed to stay alert in class.

As I hiked those two weeks and 200 miles of my 51st Birthday Hike, I had a ball. It was the most fun I have ever had.

It occurred to me that as an oldster hiker, I should be having considerably more difficulty than most of the youngsters sharing the path with me. But it was not that way.

This is not to say that I am any kind of super athlete. I'm not. I'm a desk-bound research physician at the end of a government career and at the beginning of a hiking career. I have stayed in reasonable shape, but nothing spectacular. It has been 8 or 9 years since I last played basketball with my kids–too much knee pain. I can run a mile and a half in 12 minutes–good enough to pass muster in the Air Force–but not good enough to do a respectable 5 km fun run any more.

I have personally resolved to do my best to prepare not to fail. To that end I have thought long and hard about how to get myself ready for the trail before every hike. I have practiced or experimented with technique and equipment in the safety of small overnight hikes, and then on longer hikes. Finally, I used them for a full two-week hike–successfully.

6 A Wildly Successful 200-Mile Hike

The example I leave is simple. If what I am doing in my hike is working, I keep doing it. If it is not working, then I take on the responsibility to find a better way, and then a better way after that.

My methods and ideas in this book are not the only way to hike the trail. I don't want to scold or scare anyone to hike like I do. Nevertheless, I do hope this book will prompt others to find successful ways to hike, too.

A note on geography: The book's genesis is my experience walking on the Appalachian Trail. But the book's usefulness is not entirely limited to the AT. The lessons I've learned apply to many other trails. But some of the ideas are specific to the AT. A good example would be my water management system to maintain good hydration. On the southern AT, I can generally expect at least one good water source every five miles, and certainly every ten miles. There are a lot of trails in the western part of the US where this sort of assumption would be suicidal. Water stops can be spread much more thinly than in the rain forest of the southeast US.

Perspective, Perspiration, and Perseverance: My perspective is more complicated than that of many of the people I meet. I am a physician, an engineer, and a researcher. Those are complementary backgrounds to bring to the problems of long distance hiking.

I received my medical degree in 1979 and have had three careers as a physician. I started practice as a family practice doc in northern Kentucky. Within a few years, I entered the Air Force and became an Aerospace Medicine specialist. This gave me credentials in preventive medicine as well as clinical medicine. As part of my administrative research career, it became possible for me to go back to school and earn a master's degree in Electrical Engineering. Through this, I developed an appreciation for the organized way in which engineers approach problems.

Finally, I was given the superb opportunity to invent, plan, and carry out my own research program. I learned to suspect assumptions and what everyone else already believed.

So, when I take my perspective to a problem, like blisters, I try to think about it like a clinical doc, a prevention specialist, an engineer, and a research physician. I am interested in relieving pain, using hiking poles, making the most of rest breaks, and showing that all these measures work together.

My Hiking Philosophy: My request to all I meet on the trail, and my blessing, is that they *walk well*. Walking well involves purpose, preparation, traveling on foot, and having fun going somewhere with integrity. I'll have a little more to say about this later, but there is no attempt here to get anyone to walk my way. I have no desire for anyone else to think the way I do nor to hike in the way I have discovered works for me.

8 A Wildly Successful 200-Mile Hike

At the same time, if a reader of this book finds one of my experiences useful, then I will rejoice. I will especially rejoice if I learn about it in an email or at a campsite.

A friend of mine has wisely proposed from his experience that people who have a philosophy of hiking succeed at their hiking more often than people who have not considered why they are walking in the woods. People who don't know why they are hiking often find no reason to continue. So I have a responsibility, if I am to walk well, to be able to describe my philosophy. That sounds academic, but it really is not. It really is quite simple.

At the most basic level, my philosophy is all about learning and having fun. I believe the one almost always leads to the other. At one higher level of inspection, I enjoy traveling by foot. I think I was born thinking it is wonderful to participate in what our 18th century ancestors experienced as they crisscrossed the country on walking trails. I like to be self-reliant and carry what I need on my back. For me, hiking is about travel, and not very much about camping.

Someday, I hope I can meet many of the people who read these words. I savor the opportunity to hear stories of your travels. And I earnestly hope each and every hiker who longs to walk a long distance finds the time and will to try. I hope without ceasing, that some will have a Wildly Successful 200-Mile Hike.

Without much more ado, it is time to say:

Walk Well,
Rick Allnutt, MD
AT Trail Name "Risk"

March 2005
Beavercreek, Ohio

10 A Wildly Successful 200-Mile Hike

Chapter 2

Blisters and Chafing
The Bedfellows of Friction

Blisters

Rubbed Raw in Rainbow Springs: A young man was sitting at a picnic table at Rainbow Springs Campground. His boots were off, and he had a dozen angry, oozing red blotches the size of fingernails on his toes, the back of his heel, and even on the top of his foot. Each one was the base of a broken blister that formed in the first 100 miles of his Appalachian Trail hike.

When I talked with him, he was wondering if he could get to Gatlinburg, where he planned on buying a new set of boots. Gatlinburg is another 100 miles up the trail. I heard that he left the trail just a few days later, well before reaching Gatlinburg.

What's This, Mama? I have known something about blisters since I was a child. It was a new pair of school shoes that caused my first foot blister. I remember very clearly wishing that I did not have to wear that pair of leather shoes with the stiff heel cup. Sometimes, even now, when breaking in a new pair of shoes or boots, that memory comes back. Fortunately, I've learned about blisters in my operational medicine training.

12 A Wildly Successful 200-Mile Hike

The blisters I am concerned with in a 200-mile hike are those all-too-common, round or oval, fluid-filled problem children of the feet and hands. While there are a great number of unusual causes for blisters (sunburn, frostbite, chemical burns from shoes) the most common cause is friction.

Blisters are part of every sport and every sort of work that involves the hands or the feet *and* the combination of friction and sweat. Foot blisters form when the skin's thick epidermis separates between two layers and fluid seeps into the void to cause the formation of a fluid-filled sack.

That little blister sack may have some protective value. Over the short term, it allows the skin's outer surface and those deeper layers to be separated by a lubricating fluid that prevents damage to the lower layers near the true dermis. However, my experience is that the protective value of a blister is quickly overcome by pain when friction continues and the blister breaks.

Needles in a Boot: I have been on a hike where a blister became the overwhelming center of my thought process for several days. This was a pain that felt like four sharp needles hammered partway through the heel of a boot so the ends stuck into my skin with every uphill step. It grabbed and kept my attention. I have also been on hikes when the only foot pain I have had was a tired sort of ache of all the bones and muscles of my foot–righteously earned by completing a twenty-plus mile day.

Blisters and Chafing 13

What is the difference between these hikes? Blisters. That bad blister was the result of my denying/ignoring the cause of blisters, and hiking on, when I could have done something to fix it early.

The cause of foot blisters involves friction and moisture. Friction comes from what the foot is pressed against and shear forces. Moisture comes from sweat and whatever water enters the shoe or boot.

Shear forces! "Good doctor, what do you mean by shear forces?"

When I take a step on the Appalachian Trail, it is usually uphill or down. It is not a flat surface, but is slanted, bumpy, or otherwise contorted. As I transfer weight to my foot, my foot is pressed against the bottom or side of the boot and has a tendency to want to slide against that surface. This causes a shear force between my foot and the boot.

In addition, each time I take a step, my foot moves inside the boot. There is motion between my heel and the material that makes up the heel of the boot. There is relative motion between my foot and the top of the toe box. There may be motion between the bony lumps of my ankle and the boot or shoe as well.

14 A Wildly Successful 200-Mile Hike

These shear forces are affected by the amount of boot or shoe I am wearing (high boot vs. trail runner), the fit of the footwear, and the socks I am wearing.

The shear forces act on the skin, but the many layers of the "dead" epidermis are not a homogeneous material. Much like tree rings, the layers were laid down over time affected by different physical factors. Primarily, they were affected by how much walking I was doing when they were forming. Some layers are thicker, and some thinner. Some are stuck to the other layers better and some not so well.

What will happen, given enough shear force (and moisture as detailed below) is that one of the epidermal layers will separate from its neighbor and my body will begin to fill that space up with fluid. A blister is born.

The blister may be a small nubbin at the corner of a callus, like I sometimes get on the edge of my big toe's callus. It can be in the layers of the callus of the back of the heel, or the skin of the outside edge of my little toe. I can tolerate small blisters fairly well if they stay within control, and especially if they do not break. But some blisters can be ruinous. PapaJohn Kennedy, a hiking partner in 2004, described a previous year's hike ending blister. Hiking from Stecoah Gap toward Fontana, North Carolina John lost the whole thick callus on the bottom of the balls of both feet during the long steep descent into Fontana. This was on Day One of a planned month-long section hike planned from Stecoah Gap to Damascus, Virginia. It ended his hike.

Water, Water Everywhere: Moisture is a critical ingredient for the formation of blisters. There is such a thing as just the wrong amount of moisture. Dry feet tend not to blister. Soaking wet feet tend not to blister either, though the skin can be rubbed off by friction from the outside.

Just the wrong amount of moisture–the right amount of moisture for blister formation–is frequently present inside shoes. Sometimes the wetness is due to rain or stepping in a stream. Other times it comes from slogging through high grass wet with last night's rain or this morning's dew. But most of the time, the wrong amount of wetness comes from sweating feet.

It is said by some that blisters require friction, moisture, and warmth. Since I have had blisters on cold feet in sandals, I don't believe the last requirement is necessary. However, warm feet sweat even on dry days. Unfortunately, my feet sweat just the wrong amount, making blisters a continual problem to be prevented.

Preventing blisters is not impossible, but it has taken me longer to work out a solution to blisters than any of the other major problems encountered in a 200-mile hike. In this section, I'll go through what I have tried, what has worked, and what has not worked.

16 A Wildly Successful 200-Mile Hike

I place great value on preventing blisters. I would much rather prevent a blister than treat one. However, hiking always puts me "in harm's way" when it comes to possible blister formation. This has led me to explore options and try a number of approaches to blister prevention. The following sections detail the findings.

Light Trail Runners – Ray Jardine's excellent book, *Beyond Backpacking*, makes a case for wearing light trail runners while hiking with a lightweight pack. I have hiked about a hundred miles in lightweight running shoes. They feel great as long as the trail is dry. However, they get wet in the rain and stay wet for about a day after getting soaked. Unlike Ray's experience of them drying in just a few hours after soaking, it has been my AT experience that they tend to stay wet for the rest of any hiking day during which they get wet.

Part of the problem with trying to dry out running shoes is that their insides are often padded with open cell foam just under the soft cloth liner. This open cell foam absorbs water like a sponge and holds on to the water for a long time.

Attempting to avoid the problems of water that enters from the outside, I tried the next shoe:

GORE-TEX Trail Running Shoes – I actually have about 200 walking miles in these shoes—more than any other shoe. They work great when the weather is dry, or even when it is raining a bit. They are especially dry when wearing gaiters. Unfortunately, their water resistance was overcome by two different exposures. As can be expected, when splashing in water almost as deep as the top of the shoe, water gets over the top of the shoe and soaks my feet. This has happened even when wearing gaiters. For this reason, sometimes I tried to stop hiking during the worst of the passing of a summer thunder shower, waiting for the water level in the trail's puddles to drain away before continuing. However, this strategy is not effective during all-day rainy periods. The shoes also failed when slogging through wet grass in the Smoky Mountains. Many of the trails in the southern Smoky Mountains are covered with ankle- or knee-high grass, fallen over across the trail. After a rain or when soaked with morning dew, this grass wipes across shoes and quickly soaks them. My toes were quickly squishing in puddles of water inside my GORE-TEX trail runners when I walked through fields of wet grass.

Sandals – I have tried two different brands of trail sandals. Chaco sandals have worked very well to prevent blisters. When the trail is dry enough to wear socks, the sandals give enough support to cross even the worst "rock gardens" on the trail. When I need to cross a knee-high stream, my feet and the sandal straps dry within an hour after getting out of the water. I have walked more than a hundred miles in sandals and have never had a blister in the Chacos. But sandals have their own problems outside the blister problem. I have had some problems with heel callus cracks while wearing my Chacos. I am able to control this by applying some cooking oil to the edge of the callus once a day.

Walking in sandals takes more care on my part. More than in any other sort of footwear I have worn, I need to carefully consider each footstep. On muddy paths, I look for rocks and hop from one to the next. On paths through the woods, I have developed a technique of stepping down and not swinging my feet forward, especially through leaves, where sharp sticks can impale them. In addition, I watch carefully where I put my hiking poles down. I know it would take time for my foot to heal if I poked a foot with the sharp tip of my pole.

I have had significant near misses of damage to my foot from sharp sticks poking into the top of my foot. More than once I have torn a sock when a stick jabbed into the top of my foot. I have also scraped my foot with the end of my trekking pole once when I stumbled.

Jungle Boots – These boots were designed for soldiers mucking around in swamps. Instead of being designed to keep feet dry, they allow water to enter and then quickly drain out of holes in the instep. I slogged through the aftermath of a hurricane in these boots–36 hours of constant rain–often walking on trails up to two inches deep with run-off. The boots were quite effective in preventing blisters. Though my feet were often soaked, blisters did not form. In addition, the boots eliminated one of the problems of the

Jardine inspired trail runners. They are tall enough to keep all the small sticks and stones from getting into the shoes–a common occurrence in trail runners.

Leather Vasque GORE-TEX Boots – my latest attempt at keeping my feet dry and comfortable on the trail. This pair of boots is my most comfortable solution yet for the prevention of blisters. I have only walked 100 miles in them, but so far have had comfortable feet and no blisters.

The "Ah Ha!" moment when I decided to get the leather-hiking boots was on an overnight hike in the Adirondacks. I had been spending a long day rock hopping to keep my sandals out of the trail goop. I was tired of the process. The trail was one long gully filled with rotting leaves and interspersed with big rocks. I was wearing sandals and socks. Keeping those socks clean and dry was one long balancing act. Near the end of the day, I was passed by all manner of hikers, each wearing full hiking boots. Instead of rock hopping, they were able to walk between the rocks, with dry feet. Looked good to me.

I suppose that hiking in boots is a lazy way to hike. While needing to be careful about each foot's placement, I don't have to be quite as careful. Instead of worrying about letting a half-inch of mud get over the sole of my sandal or trail runner, I am able to walk quickly and easily down the middle of the trail. How Vasque boots work in the long term, especially with days of rain in a row, is something I do not yet know. Look for the answer in my next book!

Oh Lord! Will my feet ever stop hurting? Regardless of the type of footwear, I have found it helpful to take rest breaks for blister prevention. Many of the body's organ systems do well with short rest breaks while I am hiking. Preventing blisters on my skin is a part of this overall strategy.

When I begin hiking in the morning, I try to guess how long it will be until I reach the first shelter, road crossing, or trail crossing. As mileposts between that major marker and my starting point, I divide up the distance into segments about an hour long. I do my best to keep moving for each of those hours, keeping my pack on my back. As the time for an hourly rest gets close, I begin to look for a pretty overlook, a comfy-looking rock seat or a fallen log. I usually find one within a few minutes, take my pack off and sit down.

Carrying a little scrap of waterproof silnylon or Tyvek in my pocket, I usually put it down on the surface I will be sitting on, which is almost always wet. Sometimes I use my hat for the same purpose.

The next thing I do is to take off my footwear, including my socks. I want to give my feet air to breathe. If my socks are wet, I change them out for a drier pair. After a minute or so, I put my shoes back on and begin to get ready to walk again. Sometimes I pull out my journal or Native

American flute to take up a couple more minutes enjoying the spot. Sometimes I pull out the GORP bag (Good Old Raisins and Peanuts) to begin snacking my way through lunch.

These 5-minute-long, hourly stops are the best protection I can give my feet. They allow my skin to breathe, and usually to dry. A rest break gives me the opportunity to take a look at my foot's skin and see if any new hot spots are developing–or worse–any early blister formation.

Gliding Home: Another successful prevention strategy for blisters is skin lubrication. During the hourly breaks, if I find a red area or a small blister, the best treatment I can use is something to decrease friction. One of the coolest new products I have found for this purpose is a stick form of lubrication called Bodyglide®.

I first heard of Bodyglide from other hikers who used it for chafing irritation between their legs. However, during one of the first days of a long hike from Springer Mountain to Clingman's Dome, I was puzzling about how to treat a blister that formed on my little toe during a long descent. I was using the Bodyglide for chafing and saw that the label read "prevents chafing and blisters."

I tried it for the blister on my toe and it worked magic. The blister never broke and over several days my body slowly absorbed the fluid in it.

22 A Wildly Successful 200-Mile Hike

I have had much better success with treating blisters on my toes with Bodyglide than on my heels. With those blisters, the lubrication is rubbed off the skin by my sock and is not as effective.

Layers, and more layers: A much better solution for friction on a heel is multiple layers of cloth, and sometimes the use of a piece of duct tape. Whenever I feel any irritation of my heel, I try to do something to make several layers that can rub against one another without rubbing on my skin. At a minimum this means two layers of socks. I have found that a simple way to add one more layer over my heel is to fold the thin liner sock back over my heel, creating two layers of liner sock under the thicker backpacking sock.

When layers of cloth are not enough, it can be useful to use a piece of duct tape to protect the skin from rubbing. Duct tape can be useful, but it is difficult to get it to stick well, especially if my foot is already moist. More than once, I have had some difficulty removing the duct tape from an irritated area at the end of the day without peeling off the top of a blister. For that reason, I like to take a small circle of duct tape and stick it to the sticky inside of the larger, protective patch and put the duct tape on so that this circle is centered where I think it is possible a blister may form later. Of course, if a blister has already formed, I do this carefully to ensure the top of the blister not being pulled off by the duct tape later in the hiking day.

Practice makes Perfect: Beyond all these prevention techniques is the simple act of getting feet used to walking. Blisters occur when skin not used to friction is overused. I find that one of the best methods to prevent blisters is to walk, building up distances slowly. This walking and hiking is done in the shoes used for the hike. I think it is fine for the walking to cause some irritation of the feet. That irritation leads to formation of thicker skin and resistance to blisters if not overdone before the skin adapts to the walking.

One other advantage to hardening my feet by walking is the confidence I build up in my footwear. I usually go through an increasingly difficult walking and hiking regime before trusting a pair of shoes or boots for a longer hike.

The first step is to walk around the house in the footwear. I notice whether there are any really uncomfortable spots that make the shoe/boot a "no-go" from the beginning. I walk up and down stairs. I will even walk on the edges of the stairs, simulating severe downhill and uphill slopes. This allows me to see if my toes jam into the front of the boots and what the heel feels like when it is supporting my weight. This step in the house is important, because shoes which make it out my front door are much more difficult to return to a store.

If walking in my house is not sufficient for me to make sure the shoe is a "keeper," I sometimes have taken the shoes to the shopping mall and walked around there for a while to persuade myself that I can either live with or can't live with these shoes.

Once I have decided to keep the shoes, I treat them as though there is no possibility of return (unless they fall apart in regular use.) If they are leather, I treat them with conditioner to soften the uppers. Trail runners get treated with Scotch Guard or another silicone treatment to make them water resistant. If they have a tag which irritates my foot as the Chaco Sandals did–off it comes!

I often wear a pair of hiking shoes or boots every day during the weeks before a hike. It is important for the shoes to fit very well and to mold to every bump on my feet and ankles. Daily use is the only way I have ever found to marry my feet to my shoes.

A Shoe's Sweet Dreams: Keeping shoes dry and clean-smelling decreases the growth of septic bacteria. An overgrowth of bacteria can cause problems with blisters and the health of the foot's skin. The only way I have found to be effective in keeping shoes smelling decent is to remove the source of moisture the shoe bacteria depend upon. This also helps to promote the health of the foot's skin covering.

I first learned this from my son, who was investigating a similar topic–stinky athletic shoes.

A Science Project: *William (trail name: Crow) has been doing experiments for a high school science fair competition. He is finding ways to deal with smelly athletic shoes. Athletic shoes and hiking boots have much in common. They are filled with sweaty feet and seldom have a chance to dry out completely. Both can develop an absolutely terrible smell if allowed to remain wet.*

Crow did some Internet searching for cures to smelly shoes and discovered a reference to the use of kitty litter in sports shoes.

He did an experiment involving many of his teammates' basketball shoes. Into one of the shoes he would place a sock full of kitty litter before going to bed. He did nothing to the other shoe. The next morning, he removed the kitty litter sock and presented the two shoes to his odor judges–my wife (trail name EllieD) and me. After testing this approach on shoes belonging to 15 people, it was clear that the kitty litter treated shoes were significantly better smelling and drier than the untreated shoes.

From this, I learned how important it is to dry out the inside of a shoe or boot every day.

26 A Wildly Successful 200-Mile Hike

Each night–on the trail or at home–I make sure to remove the shoe insert and let the footwear dry completely. I do not carry kitty litter on the trail (too heavy) but the experiment did teach me the importance of thoroughly drying my shoes. I have also learned to not buy shoes which have non-removable inserts. It takes too long for these shoes to dry.

Some hikers have suggested treating feet before a hike by rubbing them with alcohol or other concoctions prior to hiking. I have not tried this, nor can I think how it might help. At least one hiker, the venerable Earl Schaffer, became so discouraged with his blisters that he decided to toughen his feet by taking his socks off and pouring sand in his boots for a while. I think the amount of abrasion that could result from this would keep most people from attempting it.

I think it is far better to work-harden my feet by slowly increasing mileage and getting my feet used to hiking. This is the best preventative of all. The goal is to form callus instead of a blister. It is a great and noble ideal and can be a wonderful way to get ready for a long hike, especially if the mileage is on backpacking trails and in parks and places where I can think, and pray, and dream.

Doctor, what can I do? I have not always been successful preventing blisters. When prevention does not work, it is time to treat the blister. Hopefully the treatment will get me back to hiking as soon as possible and without long-term problems with my feet.

Blisters and Chafing 27

In its earliest form, the blister begins as a hot spot. I try to stay attuned to some of my body's aches and pains. When there is little I can do about a pain, sometimes I am able to block the pain and move on. However, with blisters, it is much better to deal with the problem as soon as it becomes noticeable. That first awareness of friction is the hot spot.

One of the few reasons I will stop before an hourly break is to look at the painful spot, and to do something about it. I have been "burned" in the past when I let a hot spot go until the next rest stop–when the hot spot had become a blister.

Blisters don't just happen. They are something I cause. Blistering is a process, not an injury event. Since blisters are bad, there is no reason for me to allow a blister to expand and break. There is always something to do which will stop the blister process: resting, changing socks, changing shoes, adding some padding, changing the tightness of the shoe with laces. Almost anything is better than letting a blister get larger and larger and then break. My foot *will* feel worse once the blister breaks. The broken blister may become infected and an infection may end a hike.

Hot spots need to be treated in some way to decrease friction or moisture or both. Often the treatment comes down to applying a piece of duct tape or moleskin over the irritated spot so that friction does not continue. During the summer, when feet are already pretty warm and sweaty,

28 A Wildly Successful 200-Mile Hike

duct tape sometimes does not stick very well. This can be worked out by using a very good quality duct tape, or by using moleskin or its cousin, medical foam tape. Whenever I apply any of these treatments, I always look for the underlying cause. Is the problem moisture or is it friction? Which one can most easily be modified? I also apply a small patch the size of the central red part of the hot spot against the sticky part of the tape. This patch is turned so that the sticky part of the two pieces stick to each other and the skin does not have the sticky glue against it. That way, if a blister does form, there will not be sticky tape to remove from the thin skin on top of a blister.

I have treated both hot spots and blisters by changing shoes. I have started carrying a very lightweight pair of moccasins for camp life at the end of the day. There have been times when I dearly missed not having the sandals with me–a half pound for the pair–as a break from my regular hiking shoes or boots. Having a pair of sandals also gives an alternative set of foot wear for fording streams, leaving the regular boots dry and less likely to cause blisters.

One effort to treat a blister was based on my lacking any tape and having a pair of boots that were eating my left heel like a crocodile. Having tried all the things I could think of, I finally started thinking about ways to create a layer of slippery friction reduction. The answer I came up with was to place a layer of slippery plastic between two layers of socks. The plastic I chose was the wrapper from a packet of Pop Tarts. This gave me many miles of service over three days. It was easier to keep the wrapper in place with some duct tape by completing a loop that ran from the heel (wrapper) around the front of my foot (tape) and back to the heel. In this way, I could tape the piece of wrapper to the outside of my liner sock and the outer sock would slide against the inner sock with almost no friction.

Treating a fully formed blister requires some judgment and experience. The skin layer on the top of a blister is one of the best bandages the blister can have. With blisters on the toes, I have been successful in coating the blister with a skin lubricant. In most cases, this is enough to keep the blister from getting larger and to keep it from breaking. If the cause of the blister can be found and fixed (tight shoes usually) then the blister will slowly absorb its fluid over a period of several days. Weeks later, the old blistered skin will peel off without pain.

Some blisters are going to break. In one case, I had a very tense blister of the top of my great toe. It was due to wet sandal material rubbing on my toe during a 40-mile, two-day binge of hiking–my first section hike of the AT. I successfully treated that blister by cleaning the skin, making a small opening in the blister, draining the fluid, and then putting a couple drops of super glue in the blister sack. I held the sack tightly closed for about a minute and it was sealed with superglue. While this really stung, it did stay tightly closed for the next 3 days, until a new layer of skin formed inside, on the base of the blister.

The classic treatment of a broken blister is to carefully remove the broken top of the blister with a pair of scissors. I have found this works out better if I wait until the end of hiking for the day and my foot will have several hours of rest to dry the newly open skin. I usually leave the floppy roof of a blister until I have time to wash my foot and care for it without hurry. There may be some advantage to putting a dab or a drop of antibiotic at the hole so that some of it gets in the blister. It may decrease the risk of infection–the only way a blister can give any real trouble that can last more than a day or two.

The good news about treating blisters is that the body will eventually fix most blister problems almost regardless of treatment. I try to remember that while blisters can really hurt, they are almost always self-healing and can be worked through to the end of a long hike. It may take a couple days of rest, or shorter-than-average days, but blisters should not require me to abandon a long hike.

Chafing

When I woke up at Neil's Gap and began packing for the day's hike, IT was still there. Each step caused a little pain. In the back of my mind was a nagging fear that each and every step would cause a little pain all day long. That pain adds up. Beyond that, I was worried that it would get worse and worse all day.

The pain I was turning over in my mind was a tiny area of chafing. It had bothered me on and off for the last two days. I treated it with a lubricant several times each day, but it had not healed up overnight.

From reading other's comments in shelter logs, chafing was a topic of obsessive concern by several hikers. Comments like "Chafing still a bother" and later "FINALLY the chafing seems to be getting better" were common. The worst of the comments were like the following, "I can't stand the rawness between my legs any longer. I have to leave the trail. Maybe I'll be back in a few weeks."

What is chafing? In medical terms, it is the loss of the top layer of the epidermis of the skin, exposing the raw nerve endings of the layers below. Sometimes it affects skin under shoulder straps or the hip belts. But more often, when hikers complain of chafing, they are talking about a number of problems of the skin in and near their groin–that is the junction of the inner upper part of the thighs with the trunk, often meant to include the external genital organs.

Chafing hurts because of the loss of the outer, protective layer of the skin. The epidermis is composed of five layers. The outer layer is a densely compacted area of flat cells that are completely dead. This layer of cells is continuously shed, taking on average two weeks to move from the bottom of the layer to the top of the heap where they are rubbed off and become dust. "From dust to dust," as the preacher says during a burial, it is exactly what the outer layer of epidermis is doing from birth to the grave.

Being dead, this layer of the epidermis has no sensation and acts much like a thin glove around the sensitive part of the skin. However, if the outer layer is removed by blistering or by rubbing it off from the outside, then the nerve endings of the skin get exposed and cause pain. This kind of "rubbing raw" is most likely when skin is moist and it is not accustomed to friction.

Pain in the Rain: I was on top of Blood Mountain, talking with a couple long distance hikers who had been walking 15 miles a day with me the last couple days. We were making better time than the rest of the pack. It was warm and we had been through several rain showers during the day. One fellow had decided that it was too much of a bother to put his rain jacket on each time it began to shower. He had decided to just take his shirt off and get wet.

He was carrying a pack loaded with about 50 pounds of his most essential gear and two weeks of food. (Early in the hike, a number of hikers have not yet come to grips with the amount of gear or the amount of food to carry. See more on this topic in Chapter 5 – The One Best Idea.)

When I climbed on top of the rocks above the shelter he was complaining of his sore back. I said that my back was sore too. But muscle soreness is not what he meant. He made a quarter turn and showed me what he meant. Across both hips, he had a band about two inches wide and 8 inches long that looked like the skin had been attacked with sandpaper for several hours.

His anti-raincoat strategy had backfired on him. Because his hip belt was padded with open cell foam (read sponge) and enclosed in rough pack cloth, the pack had eaten all the way through the dead layer of his skin. The resulting blood crusted areas helped him earn the trail name Rawhide right then and there. That is just what his hips were–raw down to the red and painful base layers of skin.

Fire in the Groin: On my first multi-day AT section hike, I was wearing a pair of loose nylon swim trunks with a polyester net liner. I had experimented with them at home for months. It worked quite well to wash them by hand each evening and hang them to dry. I thought this gear technique had eliminated all chance for developing a chafing rash between my legs, and eliminated the need to carry underwear on the trail. .

It was late May in North Carolina and the days were getting hot. I started off the first day putting in big mileage–eighteen miles was way too much–and by the end of the day I began to notice an irritation where the liner rubbed against my upper thighs. I was not sure if the problem was the miles, or the dry sweat in the liner, or the cloth itself.

I was carrying some thick ointment (Desitin) that I used in an attempt to treat the areas. It was mostly a useless exercise. The bathing suit liner wiped the ointment off after only a few steps and the skin started to hurt again. It took several days for the skin to start feeling back to normal. I also knew I needed to find another way to deal with sweat and friction.

Developing an understanding: I thought my problems with chafing were a simple result of too many miles. I hoped the cure was to decrease the miles (which I needed to do for my knees as will be seen in another chapter) and that I would not need to do anything else.

Imagine my disappointment on my second section hike when the problem resurfaced. This hike was in the Virginia highlands in July. Again, at the end of the first day of hiking, both upper thighs were red and painful. My skin was covered with a salty residue that felt like sandpaper. Between my thighs and the liner brief of my swim-trunk shorts, the top layer of epidermis had been worn down by a single day's hike.

I began to think about the causes of chafing and what I might be able to do about it. Clearly, heat and sweat were involved with skin rubbing off and hurting. The formation of salt crystals on my skin and in the material of the briefs was also an ingredient. Bacteria seemed to play a part, because the accumulated sweat down in those folds smelled none too sweet. I also found that the individual hair follicles were red. Either the hair was being pulled or the follicle was reacting to the chemical and bacterial stew.

I remembered that I had similar problems when training for and running a full marathon race several years ago. That experience had a similarity to my long walks. Both cases involved heat and sweat and lots of miles.

Some say that in the adaptation process of both marathon runners and long distance hikers, these long distance travelers begin to modify their stride for maximum efficiency. Especially with the extra weight of a backpack, walkers learn to swing their feet more in front of themselves with each step, placing the foot so that it will be at the center of balance after taking a step. One result is a tendency for the hiker's upper thighs to rub more against each other than in normal daily life

This can be a problem for those with a "little extra padding" at the top of their legs. Yes, it's true, being overweight causes many problems for hikers, and chafing is one of them.

I have had problems with groin chafing in two different areas. When wearing a pair of shorts or underwear, I have the same problems with irritation of my upper thighs as is reported by many other hikers. However, when wearing a kilt,

I have chafing on a very small part of my skin, less than a half inch square. This area is right on the midline of my body. It is behind the scrotum and in front of the anal area. When it is irritated, this can be a very tender spot. For me, it stays irritated for about two days at the beginning of a hike, but is very easily kept in control with two or three simple ideas as detailed in the prevention and treatment paragraphs below. Sometimes this irritation is limited to one or two hair follicles.

The Root of Understanding: Hair roots of the skin in the groin area can cause as much problem as loss of the upper epithelial layers of skin. The hair root, or follicle, is a complex little structure. Not only does hair grow from the follicle, there are associated oil glands in the follicle. The hair socket is continually attacked by friction, moisture, salt, abrasive dirt, and growth of bacteria. This can lead to swelling, redness, and pain of the hair follicle. Of course, added to this problem in each hair follicle is the overlying irritation of the skin between each hair. The overall result can be anything from a little irritation to a three-alarm fire. This is not a pleasant situation. As with most problems, I try to prevent the problem before it gets this far.

What's rubbing me wrong? Since one primary cause of skin abrasion in the groin is clothing, a careful look at what is rubbing the skin is worthwhile.

I have worn cotton underwear while hiking. I don't like it. The briefs quickly get wet from sweat and take forever to dry. They never dry while I am

Blisters and Chafing 37

wearing them. They have seams that act as a rope against already raw skin and begin to saw through the upper portions of skin. Consequently, they are a wet cloth with irritating seams that rubs and makes all the chafing issues worse.

Boxers are not much better. They are cotton, which means they dry slowly especially when covered by other clothing. Worn under another pair of shorts or pants, they bunch up and cause little local abrasions where they get caught between the outer pants and my skin.

I've read trail reports from female hikers who swear by the comfort of panties worn inside out. This puts the smooth surface without seams on the inside against skin and the not so pretty seams on the outside. I pass their advice along for the half of the population I do not represent. It seems like it would work well.

I have successfully hiked in nylon swimming trunks. These are boxer-like trunks with a polyester brief sewn in. They can be rinsed in stream water, and put back on to dry. In very humid weather, I have even put them back on inside out to dry more quickly. I almost always carry a pair, because they make great town clothes and can be important when dealing with chafing during the first few days of a hike. There is a tendency, especially in hot weather, for salt to become encrusted in the material of the brief, making it like sandpaper, and for that to wear away at the skin of each upper leg.

38 A Wildly Successful 200-Mile Hike

The most important strategy for preventing chafing is keeping the skin clean. That salty residue I mentioned earlier really was like fine sand paper to my skin, except the "sand" was dry salt from sweat. For this reason, chafing always seems to more of a problem on warm days. How warm? Warm enough to sweat. It is also more of a problem when the skin dries and the salt forms into sharp crystals on the surface of my skin or clothing.

Cleaning several times a day just by rinsing removes the dry salt and makes the skin smoother. It also removes any bacteria that have accumulated in the grunge at the bottom of creases. Wearing a kilt makes it much easier to clean off with a cup of water dipped from a stream. It is best to walk down the trail a few yards, and then dribbling the water from the cup into one hand, it is easy to rinse off under the kilt while squatting with bent knees.

Really cleaning, that is with soap and water each evening also improves the health of my skin. This does a better job of killing the bacteria that cause irritation at the depths of the hair follicles.

OK, but what about days when that knowledge is not enough? It's true enough, I have a hard time getting through the first couple days of a hike wearing a pair of bathing trunks as shorts. Fortunately, I have a couple other tricks up my sleeve that help with chafing.

Lubrication helps. If it is not too wet or hot, talcum powder or baby powder works pretty well to both dry the skin and to make skin more slippery. I know from my medical practice that it is the talcum powder sort of baby powder that works best. Cornstarch based baby powders are exactly what fungus organisms that live in wet nooks and crannies love to eat. It makes them flourish. There is no reason to feed an organism that will strip the skin off my groin!

Another lubricant that works well is Bodyglide, also mentioned in the section on blisters. It seems to stick to the skin well and seal the skin from further wetness. At the same time, the waxy nature of the material makes even wet skin do better.

I have tried plain petroleum jelly as a lubricant without much success. It seems to rub off so quickly that I need to apply it almost constantly.

One other material I have tried is a cream sold in farm supply stores called Udder Balm. Yep, it is made for udders, but it is also labeled for use on "hands and other skin areas." What it does very well is to assist in overnight healing of areas that are chafed and chapped. It is full of lanolin, Aloe Vera, and several vitamins that promote healing.

A Kilt? You've got to be joking! Want still another defense against chafing? I've mentioned a kilt already, and it really works wonders. No joke.

40 A Wildly Successful 200-Mile Hike

I've now worn a kilt (or hiking skirt) for about 400 miles of hiking on the AT, and I can't imagine wearing anything better. Here are the standard answers to the standard questions:

> - *Am I wearing anything under it? No, if I wore anything under it, what would be the purpose of wearing the kilt?*
> - *Am I Celtic? Yes, I am descended from the Manx, on the Isle of Man.*
> - *I'm careful when I sit down.*
> - *I see you're not wearing a kilt.*
> - *No, it's nice and warm (cool).*
> - *No, no mosquito bites.*

I have found the kilt to be one of the best solutions to lots of hiking problems, but chafing was the reason I tried it. For that purpose it works great.

Even with the kilt, I still have a little chafing at the beginning of a hike with a kilt. I find it best to wear the kilt for a day, then the shorts for a day, and to alternate until my skin gets more used to the daily mileage. Once I am used to hiking, the kilt's other advantages (stays clean, convenient for rest stops, dries quickly) keep me wearing it.

The Good News: The gospel about chafing is much like that of blisters. While an occasional hiker has chafing that lasts a whole 200 miles, most people begin to get over the problem within a hundred miles. Though it can hurt with each step, there are lots of choices that will rescue a hike. Treated properly, it is normal for the body to adapt with thicker skin. As the hike continues, less and less thought needs to be spent on chafing as a problem.

The Bedfellows of Friction:

Friction injury of the skin can cause problems with either blisters (usually of the feet) or chafing. The answers I have found work to keep my skin healthy and pain free.

To avoid blisters I always try to find a way to keep my feet cool and dry. Shear forces can be controlled with choice of shoes and socks. Stopping to air out my feet once an hour helps in preventing and knowing about any need to treat a new blister. Other helps include lubrication, adjusting shoes for the right tightness, and using moleskin.

Chafing prevention and treatment includes staying clean with frequent washing, lubricants, and wearing either light breathable shorts or even better, a kilt.

In the next chapter, one of the hiker's most common, and also one of the most-difficult-to-deal-with injuries is described. When I was in the Boy Scouts, a new hiker was called "Tenderfoot." But it is not feet that cause the worst of many hikers' problems on the Appalachian Trail, it's their knees. The next chapter is devoted to youngsters and oldsters alike, it is for everyone that might have a problem with their knees. That list includes just about everyone.

42 A Wildly Successful 200-Mile Hike

Chapter 3

Knees – It's All About Prevention and Preparation

The Octopus Tree: It is a few minutes north of the sign that signifies the North Carolina and Georgia border on the Appalachian Trail. Surrounding the tree is an open grassy space. I did not sit down to enjoy the moment. Now, partway up the hill I regretted my haste. Immediately on leaving that meadow the trail ascends along the spine of a tall hill. I did not know it, but I was beginning the steepest climb of the southernmost 200 miles of the trail. It is harder than Albert Mountain, Blood Mountain, Frosty Mountain, and Tray. It is steeper than the climb out of Stecoah Gap.

I used my poles to push from behind me instead of planting them in front. It was a gut wrenching and exhausting climb. But, like all climbs, it ended. This one ended with a much more gradual ascent along a sloping trail to the ridgeline.

For me, the pain was behind me. I had taken my time and refused to clomp my way to the top in anger at the mountain. Unfortunately that is not true of everyone who poles themselves up this hill.

Wesser Descent: It is a long and steep descent from the fire tower atop Wesser to the bridge at the NOC. Miles and miles of unremitting descent greeted me after I woke at Cold Spring shelter and worked my way toward the NOC for lunch. I was dancing my way down the mountain in little steps and having a ball. I thought back to the stories I had heard from friends about this drop-off. Stories of heel blisters, and numerous stories of knees giving out were whirring through my mind as I pranced my way down and down and down toward a cheeseburger at River's End.

50th Birthday! I had decided months before not to be anywhere around my office on my 50th birthday. I had no desire to be the guest of honor at a party decked out with black crepe paper and all the tired jokes of being over the hill. Instead I decided to actually be over the hill…and then over the next one.

It was my first section hike on the AT. I walked eighteen miles that day before my birthday northbound out of Hot Springs, and then 22 miles on my birthday the following day. Toward the end of that second day, well after supper, I found myself climbing up a 1000 foot series of switchbacks to Sugar Loaf Gap. The trail included an abundance of rock steps, and I began to notice a grinding sound coming from my left knee.

I remembered that I had been lifting myself up each step with my left leg, because I was beginning to develop a blister on my right foot. I wanted to protect the right foot so the blister would not break.

Knees – It's All About Prevention and Preparation

The next morning, when I woke up at Frosty Knob and started walking down the first small hill, I found that my left knee was desperately painful. Each step felt like I had completely worn out the inside surface of the joint and that bone was rubbing on bone. Ibuprofen did not even begin to bring the pain into control. If I was going to continue it was going to be in the face of pain.

***

The Trail Community Marches on Its Knees: Knee pain is a common and really wicked problem on a 200-mile hike. It has been said that if hikers prepare to avoid knee problems, they are ready for anything the trail dishes out. They will finish their hike. However, if hikers are not prepared to prevent knee pain, their odds of finishing drop considerably.

It's my experience that most problems on a 200-mile trail can be worked out with the help of fellow hikers, with the single exception of knee pain. Knee pain does not go away in a day or two. It does not get better after a hot shower or a hot meal. It does not get better after sleeping–in fact, it is likely to be worse.

Knee pain takes at least two weeks, and more often a month, to get well. And then it comes back if proper prevention is not applied the second time. I try to remember that injury of my knee does not lead to immunity the next time around; it just makes worse injury more likely.

46 A Wildly Successful 200-Mile Hike

Primacy of Prevention: The way to deal with knees is to do everything possible to make sure they do not begin to fall apart in the first place. Fortunately, doing what is good for the knees is good for the rest of my systems too. But first, it is worth thinking about the knees from an engineering standpoint. What are the weaknesses of the design? What goes wrong? What pathology of the knee gets a hiker in trouble?

Knees 101 – An Anatomy Class "The thigh bone's connected to the leg bone." That's what the old song said. What connects the two is called the knee. The knee is a fantastically efficient, self-repairing, hinge joint. The upper and lower bones slip on each other's joint cartilage which is inside the knee joint itself. In front of the joint is a little cap of bone called the patella. It rides in a groove on the front of the knee and the back side of the patella is also covered with cartilage. The cartilage surfaces are inside a mostly collapsed sack with just a little bit of slippery lubricating fluid inside the sack.

The knee joint allows me to perform two important functions. With the muscles in the thigh, I am able to bend and straighten the knee. The hinge locks at just about 180 degrees and can not be over extended without tearing structures in the knee.

The outside walls of the knee are formed by ligaments to the left and right of the leg, just at the level of the knee. They have cool names like the MCL (Medial Co-lateral Ligament) and are

Knees – It's All About Prevention and Preparation

sometimes strained by walking, or by a fall. When a ligament is torn this is called a strain or sprain depending on how serious the injury is.

[Note: there are many other important structures and ligaments in the knee that can be injured–The cruciate ligaments etc.–but they are not normally affected by hiking as much as they are destroyed in auto accidents, falls, and football games.]

The Pulley Game: In understanding how a knee gets hurt, it is helpful to think about how a knee works. The muscles that move the knee are in the thigh. The quads on the front of the thigh attach to the patella on the front of the knee and thence to the patellar tendon which is attached to the front of the lower leg about an inch below the knee. The hamstring muscles attach through two tendons on both sides of the back of the knee to the lower leg.

If this is too much detail for some readers to absorb, it works well enough to remember that muscles moving joints are connected across the joint by tendons attached to the bone on the opposite side of the joint from the muscle.

When my hamstring muscles contract, my lower leg and my boot are lifted clear of the ground. Each lower leg weighs about 10-15 pounds and my boots are about two pounds apiece. (Moccasins are about ¼ pound apiece.) As the muscles contract, there is some strain between the surfaces of the knee.

However, the stress on my knee's inner cartilage surfaces, when my quads contract, is much greater. The pull of the quads is transferred to that spot on my tibia and the muscles have to pull hard enough to lift all my weight minus the 10-15 pounds of the lower leg, plus whatever clothing and pack I have on.

There is a tremendous pressure that develops between the surfaces of the knee and of the back of the patella against the front of the knee with each step. What's more, if the knee is deeply bent, as happens when taking a big step up, the stress between those joint surfaces increases exponentially. The pressure between the surfaces can easily be many thousands of pounds as my body weight is multiplied according to the rules of levers which we all try to forget from high school physics.

Stressed Out at Sassafras Gap: Stress for the knees is like school to a high-school senior. I don't like stress, but I know it prepares me for hard times ahead. Getting my knees ready for stress takes stress–and that's one to take home.

There are two additional problems of the knee that bother hikers. The first involves the ligaments around the knee. Tripping, falling, playing touch football, and walking on uneven, breadbox-sized rocks and slipping off a few of them can strain and stretch the ligaments.

This illness is like a strain or sprain of the ankle. The damage is actually outside the joint itself. The milder strain is most common. Most often, it can be felt with a finger as a sore spot on the middle or outside joint line on the side of the knee. If it is sensitive, a little tender-loving care can take care of the pain and keep a hiker on the trail.

After a fall, it is possible for the ligaments to be torn. This usually leads to bleeding into the joint, and what is really obvious is the inability to put any weight on the knee. This needs a doctor's attention and will mean leaving the trail for a while. There is no mistaking this pain for one of the other knee problems, except maybe for a broken bone.

I'm Sorry Sir, This Account is Overdrawn: The second and most common illness is due to overuse of the knee. The problem here is not with the ligaments on the outside of the knee joint. Instead the structures inside the knee joint are literally worn down to the bone.

What causes the knee to get worn to a frazzle is treating the knee like it can not be hurt. Simple isn't it? The first lesson the trail taught me was that my knee could be hurt. And if it got hurt it would make sure I knew it.

I hurt my knee climbing those 1000 feet into Sugar Loaf Gap and then another 500 feet to Frozen Knob. This whole climb was after supper during my second day on the trail! I was at a perfectly good shelter at 5 PM, but I had a bug in my ear to walk another 8 miles because "I was not tired yet."

My problem was that my left knee wore out before the rest of me. Even when I knew it was worn out (making creaking sounds) I still climbed another 500 feet. I was treating my knee like it could not get hurt and it taught me the lesson. I finished that section hike, two and a half days later, but every step hurt. It hurt badly.

One of the mechanisms I used to wear out my knee was to prefer one knee over the other. This is almost never a good idea. My right foot was a little tender as I began that long evening climb. I remember hundreds of 6 to 18 inch step-ups over rocks, roots, water bars, and carved steps. I lifted myself up all of them with my left knee. I was saving the right one. I was honestly surprised when my left knee started grating and giving me some pain near the top of the climb. I'd never had problems with my knees and I really and honestly believed that I could not hurt them. I was wrong.

This New Job May Seem Like a Step Down...
However, many people get themselves into more trouble going down than going up. During those days after I wore my knee out, what I discovered was that I could climb slowly without pain, but it was nearly impossible to descend pain free.

Each step down a mountainside places great stress on the knee. Think about what is happening–with knee locked, I bounce down a step, hammering my leg with the full weight of my body and pack. The way I used to hike, I'd do this over and over and over.

I see hikers do this all the time. It's a ballet: Big steps, Packs jangling, Dust rising. It feels good to be making big miles down the hill. It works if the hill is a mile long. Before long, the stress decreases as the climbing slows down the hiker. But some hills are much bigger and can be trouble. I used to be the most jangling hiker on the trail. It lasted 2 days. I wore out my knee. I had much to learn, as it turned out, before I could successfully walk 200 miles without knee pain. But by then I had cheated. I had built a prescription for my knees and filled it. I was taking it every day.

Rx: Healthy Knee Formula – Here are the elements of my personal knee prescription:

- *Mileage Limit – realistic expectations*
- *Spread the Load – left right left…*
- *Weight Limit – forgetting the pack is there*
- *Hiking poles – two of them*
- *Medication – glucosamine and ibuprofen*
- *Dancing down hills – Shuffle step*

In the sections below, I will flesh out each part of the Healthy Knee Formula.

52 A Wildly Successful 200-Mile Hike

Where do you think you're going so fast? A mileage limit has proven to be an important part of keeping my knees healthy. The hardest part was dealing with unrealistic expectations during my first section hikes on the AT.

I knew that I could walk about four miles an hour. I have been walking that fast for years, back and forth from friends' houses, to appointments, to college, and between buildings on the Air Force base where I had worked.

I knew that Ray Jardine clearly described a good hiking day as: eleven miles between breakfast and an early lunch, eleven miles from lunch to dinner, and eleven miles before setting up camp. With no one to slow me down, I figured that I should be able to accomplish the same schedule. I had begun to pack ultralight, and test walks in Ohio parks were right on the money for speeds necessary to walk that far.

Then the reality of those first section hikes on the Appalachian Trail set in. It immediately became obvious that I was not going to walk 33 miles in a day. So I set about to walk at least 12-14 hours... What else did I have to do? Besides, I was getting exercise points back at my job for each hour of backpacking–four points per hour.

Ohio trails (Zaleski State Forest) are not the same as AT trails for anyone who has not noticed. In Ohio, a 300-foot climb is memorable. On the AT, a 3000-foot climb is noted. In addition, the path surface on much of the AT is very tricky. Rock

Knees – It's All About Prevention and Preparation 53

gardens of bread-loaf-sized loose rocks abound, with many covered with slick green algae. The first few times I timed myself between known points and calculated my mile per hour speed, I was crestfallen. I could hardly believe my progress was so slow.

For both reasons, elevation change and the condition of the pathway, my hiking speed decreased from four miles an hour to something between one and two miles an hour.

But worse, even with the slower speeds, I found that my knees were just not up to putting in the 16 hour days I had planned. I could almost tough it out for a day or two, but not for the two weeks it takes to walk 200 miles. I badly needed to change my expectations.

What I have discovered since those early walks is an expectation of beginning a walk with 12-15 mile days. Assuming I am in good hiking form, I move toward 18-20 mile days after a week of hiking. What this really means, is hiking about 8-10 hours a day. When planning a trip, my rough rule of thumb is to plan on 15 miles a day or 100 miles a week. That has given me enough time to complete walks without being late getting back to work, and sometimes I've been able to come back to my house a day early on longer section hikes. For the 200-mile trip of this book, I finished the walk from Springer to Clingman's Dome in 13 days.

54 A Wildly Successful 200-Mile Hike

Left Right Left Right... I must be a little slow on the uptake. It is hard for me to remember to take steps alternating between my right and left feet. On steep sections of the trail, where water bars or steps have been placed by the trail crews, my inclination is to take a whole section of the hill lifting myself up each step with the same leg.

It goes something like this:

> *Left up! Shuffle, shuffle, shuffle, Left up! Shuffle, shuffle, shuffle.*

Or even worse:

> *Bang down with my right! Step, step, step. Bang down with my right!*

I wrongly tend to use the same foot to hoist my self up each step or to bounce down each step. I think this is because I turn for the large steps so that I lead with my hip, either up or down hill.

My prescription for not injuring one knee is to spread the load and alternate the stresses. It takes a new dance step, especially when headed down a hill.

> *Quarter turn left. Step down with right foot. Walk to next step. Quarter turn right. Step down with left foot. Walk to the next step...*

Knees – It's All About Prevention and Preparation

Uphill, I concentrate on momentarily stopping below each water bar or root and mentally alternating right and left as I climb a stepped hillside.

This alternating of knees continues even when one or the other gets a little tender. If knee tenderness continues for more than a few minutes, it is time for a break. If a break does not clear up the problem, it's time for a nap. If a nap does not fix it, it is time to stop for the day. (Camping hammocks are useful for taking naps or camping in the middle of long climbs.)

Hey! Weight for me! Fifteen pounds is a magic backpack weight. When I keep my pack weight to this weight, I don't think about my pack at all. It is a piece of clothing, not a burden to bear. A fifteen-pound pack is also magic for my knees. It turns an expedition into a walk in the park. It turns a mountain into a tall hill.

Backpack weight is not the only weight I carry around. Like most 50-year-olds, I tend to carry around Thanksgiving turkey and Christmas ham as well. I weighed 165 pounds when I was 30 and now I weigh 200.

Long-distance hiking has the tendency to be self-correcting. On the 200-mile hike, my weight dropped from 200 to 192. I liked the trend, though it cannot be continued indefinitely. On a month long hike, I would hope to either start or achieve a weight of about 180 and then maintain it.

Knees appreciate any loss of weight before a hike. Each step is a strain on their anatomy that takes my weight and applies a multiplying factor to that weight, which is then applied to the joint surfaces. If the starting weight is lower, the joint surface stress ends up being smaller by that same multiplying factor.

The Exorcist: Exercise before a long hike, or between long hikes is essential preparation. I like to mix running and upper body strengthening. By long habit, I run about two miles three times a week. There are many purposes fulfilled by my jogging.

Running toughens my ankles, knees, and feet. I find this especially useful in decreasing foot pain on long hiking days. My ankles stay strong, especially if a portion of the running is outdoors on grass and uneven ground. Calluses are maintained for the prevention of blisters, and my cardiovascular system gets a good work out too.

Another good way I have prepared for hiking the AT is to hike near home. Unlike running, it is possible to do these training hikes while carrying the same equipment I would be carrying on the AT. And for some purposes, hours on my feet are a more important preparation than miles I have traveled. Day hiking allows me to put in many hours of exercise without becoming worn out prematurely.

Knees – It's All About Prevention and Preparation

The effect of regular running or day hiking on knees is remarkable. It prepares me for beginning a hike with 12-15 mile days instead of the 5-6 mile days which many (even young) AT hikers start with. However, if time pressures or just plain laziness keeps one from preparing ahead of time, all is not lost. Actual hiking the trail is still the best exercise to prepare for hiking the AT.

If I ever find myself physically unprepared for a long hike, I will begin anyway. The difference will be that I will make small mileage for a week or two of the hike. Starting at five or six miles for a few days, then gradually increasing over a two week period, until I can comfortably walk 15-20 mile days, is a time proven approach to the trail.

The Whole Earth Revolves Around its Poles: I grew up walking with a hiking stick. Picking up a stick to walk with from the side of the trail was just the thing to do. When I was living in Germany in the late 1980s, and vacationed in the Alps, some of the Swiss walkers were using a lightweight hiking stick by a company I had never heard of called Leki. (Now Leki is world famous for their hiking and trekking poles.) I bought one of their "Lightsticks" and fell in love with its clickity-clack on the rocky mountain trails. I began my first section hike of the AT with that pole, but quickly discovered that a majority of the thru-hikers on the trail were using pairs of poles by Leki and other companies.

I usually ask questions of my fellow hikers about their equipment. I ask what their most important piece of equipment is and what they have found to be most useless. On that first hike, a young man going by the name of FugiBoots told me that he believed the only reason he had been able to walk the 300-plus miles he had already come, was because of his two hiking poles. An Israeli girl named Patience seconded the thought.

I picked up a wooden stick on that trip as a second pole and it really did seem to help with the knee pain I was having. One of the plans I made to prevent knee pain for my return to the trail on the next section hike was to come back with two poles. I bought a pair of poles the first chance I had and I have hiked with two poles on the AT ever since.

A pair of poles lessens the impact on my knee when stepping down a long step. The poles also help me when I need help to pull myself up big steps. They help me to maintain my balance on slippery piles of rocks and to recover without falling when I trip over something in the pathway.

Doctor, What Should I Take For My Knees?
Medication for the knees during a hike is mostly for prevention. The treatment covered below is for extended rest times, not trail days.

The best-known preventive medication is ibuprofen. It works for pain, but the main gain is the ability of the drug to reduce inflammation. Whenever one of the supportive tissue systems of the body (muscle,

Knees – It's All About Prevention and Preparation

ligament, tendon, skin) gets irritated, a cascade of chemical events begins. The process is called inflammation. Inflammation is perceived as pain, redness, warmth, and swelling. Anti-inflammatory drugs like ibuprofen stop the cascade and stop all four outcomes of the irritation.

Ibuprofen does nothing to reduce the wear and tear that caused the inflammation, but it does modify the swelling as well as the pain. Since swollen tissues are more easily injured by wear and tear, taking ibuprofen reduces the risk of even more damage.

I sometimes need to remind myself that pain has a purpose. It begins to get my attention and get me to change what I am doing. So I do not take ibuprofen to be able to keep walking and cause more damage. I use it to promote return to normal during rest periods. I especially take the medication in the evening after a hard day so that it can work with the night's rest to repair any damage which accumulated during the day.

The other medication I have found to be essential to my 50-year-old knees is glucosamine. This "food supplement" is available over the counter at outrageously varying prices and doses. The scientific literature is incomplete on the benefit of glucosamine with and without one of the two drugs often combined with it: chondroitin sulfate or methylsulfonylmethane (MSM). All three have been used in veterinary practice for years to prevent or treat osteoarthritis.

From talking with a number of people, the medications work for some and do not work for others. The difference may not be genetic—glucosamine does not affect my mother's arthritis, but it does wonders for me. Personal testing is about the only way to determine if taking the medications might be worthwhile. I have concentrated on stand-alone glucosamine for myself, as this seems to prevent all the problems I had with my knees previously.

The mechanism of action for glucosamine is believed to be as a promoter of repair of cartilage, the white, slippery stuff that can be seen at the end of chicken drumstick bones. That same cartilage is on the internal surfaces of my knee and it was that same cartilage which was damaged on my 50th birthday hike.

One of the well known tricks for successfully using glucosamine to keep knees healthy is that it must be started weeks before the hike. The stuff does not act immediately. Another important point is to take enough of it to matter. It is a food supplement and has no real toxicity at high doses. Most studies have been done with a dose of 1.5 grams (1500 mg) of glucosamine a day. Anecdotally, this is a bare minimum dose for hikers.

I choose to take two grams of glucosamine a day every day. While hiking I increase the dose to 4 grams a day. At this dose, some people seem to have a little increased intestinal gas. Personally, I would rather fart some and have healthy knees, but it does not seem to be an issue for my intestinal

Knees – It's All About Prevention and Preparation

system. I tolerate the four grams without any problem. I have corresponded with thu-hikers who have taken up to six grams a day during difficult parts of the hike.

I have found prices of glucosamine ranging from $0.50 to $0.04 a gram. It pays to shop. The least expensive form I have found is in bottles of 240 tablets. Each tablet contains one gram of glucosamine. (Sam's Club, 2005)

Dancing Down Wesser: Sometimes the hill is high and the path long. From the top of Wesser Bald to a lunch date at the NOC, it was a nearly 3000 foot constant descent over six and a half miles of trail. That is real descending.

Partway down, I was thinking of lessons learned the hard way. On that first section hike of mine, somewhere near Whistling Gap, I discovered the benefit of having a bit of fun.

Since my knee hurt badly enough to make tears well up in my eyes, and I had already prayed about it, I decided to whistle down the hill instead of cursing down the hill. While whistling, I decided to also dance down the hill. I settled into a little shuffle in time to the song, using my poles as a dancing partner and prop. I was having a ball being ridiculous. About then I noticed that my knee did not hurt nearly so badly.

The scientist in me took notice. I started walking down the hill. Pain came back. I started dancing down the hill. Pain went away. Hmm....

After playing around with it, I found that taking quick little shuffling steps downhill–almost without regard for footing–felt quite tolerable. It saved my 50th birthday hike. It also saved my 200-mile hike a year later, on that long descent from Wesser. I just kept singing and shuffling and taking little steps all the way down that huge hill. I still can't sing worth anything, and my dancing is shamefully amateur, but my knees think I am the best dancer around. And they are the audience I am playing to. As it was, I made that descent and many more without knee pain.

No Pain is a Very Good Thing: I keep thinking back to Heads Up sitting there at the base of Standing Indian. His knees had exploded from the inside. They were full of inflammatory fluid. When I pressed down on his patella, it gave way and clicked into his knee surfaces a half inch away, on the other side of a water balloon that should not have been there. I knew his hike was probably over, but wished him well anyway. There is a kind of grief at seeing the end of a fellow hiker's dream.

Within a week of my catastrophic 50th Birthday Hike, I had made a four-part plan to return to the trail and keep my knees healthy with a deep defense posture. Besides staying in shape and keeping my body and pack weights down, I decided it was important to:

Knees – It's All About Prevention and Preparation

- *get a pair of hiking poles*
- *control my mileage–stop before hurting myself*
- *take glucosamine*
- *dance down the hills*

A year later, during my first 200-mile hike, my knees were never an issue, and I learned to make friends with Springer, Hawk, Gooch, Big Cedar, Granny Top, Burnett Field, Blood, Levelland....

64 A Wildly Successful 200-Mile Hike

Chapter 4

Losing the Will to Hike

A Song for the Moon: One o'clock AM and all is well... My hammock hangs next to the drop-off at the Vandeventer shelter, and the October night sky is beautifully lighted by the nearly full hunter's moon.

I've gotten up for my middle-of-the-night pee, and I am entranced by the stillness. The night is so clear that I could reach out and touch the hills on the far side of the valley. It will be a long night, with many more hours of darkness than I need to sleep, so I walk around the silent walls to the front of the shelter.

As I turn the corner, mice scurry about in their nocturnal searching for food. But this night there are no other hikers from which to gain sustenance with a trifle stolen from a pack. My own food is outside the shelter, back near my hammock, and they will not find it before the sun and daylight make them less frisky.

I sit on the edge of the shelter floor and listen into the darkness. The woods are much quieter than in mid-summer, but I can still hear the occasional night creature as it creates a rustling scurry in the dry leaves.

66 A Wildly Successful 200-Mile Hike

A great horned owl calls from across a ravine. Hearing no answer, I do my best to imitate his call. It must not be good enough, because he does not come closer. Instead he calls out again and again, probably laughing under his breath at the sound of the city-slicker, pseudo owl that has wandered into his forest.

Back near my hammock, I pull the Native American flute from the side pouch of my pack. Settling my back against a chilly rock, a low and mournful song emerges from my mind and is transmitted through my fingers and the flute into the night vapors. My breath propels the rising melody arrhythmically through the naked branches and toward the moon.

I feel one with the woods, my spirit feasting in this October forest, bathed by the hunter's light. For an hour I sit suspended between earth and sky, looking over the valley of mortals entombed in their square plastic boxes, fitfully sleeping their way through the night.

Finally, refreshed by my spiritual night walk, I lean back in my hammock, pull the quilt over my chilled shoulders, and in my rocking bed, I fall asleep.

Much of my experience in the woods is mental and spiritual. The more time and experience I have in the forest, the less it feels like wilderness and the more it feels like home.

Thirty Percent Solution? There is a saying in the hiking community that hiking is thirty percent physical and seventy percent mental. Simply stated, all that preceded in this booklet about blisters and chafing and knee pain, plus all the other equipment issues combined are just a small part of what it takes to walk in the woods.

It takes dedication, a dream, and a good attitude to successfully walk a long way. It helps to consider that there will be rough times, but there will be enough fun to keep going. This helps me to meditate on how I will act when I am discouraged.

I like to think of wet days and disappointments like pepper and salt. By themselves, they are irritating, but combined with the rest of the hiking fare, they make the whole hike much more memorable. Besides, there is an opportunity for learning to make peace with the woods and with myself whenever it is raining:

> *"There is something to be learned from a rainstorm. When meeting with a sudden shower, you try not to get wet and run quickly along the road. But...you still get wet. When you are resolved from the beginning, you will not be perplexed, though you still get the same soaking."*
> *- Yamamoto Tsunetomo*

It is a matter of attitude, and losing my resentment of the weather God gives us today. Much of the hiking experience is like this.

Wanted: Hiker/Walker: I ran across a job description for an outdoors guiding job. Maybe the job of "Hiker" is a little like the guide job. This is what it had to say about job conditions:

> *Frequent exposure to heat, cold and wet/humid conditions; continual field work; moderate mental effort is required daily; great mental effort is occasionally required; moderate mental pressure exists due to exposure to interpersonal conflicts; moderate physical exertion is necessary; hours worked are 24 hours a day, 7 days a week.*

(I modified the hours worked to be more realistic.)

Hiking requires the kind of person that can enjoy all those conditions. Not everyone does. However, not everyone who gets a hankering to go hiking has considered the actual surroundings they will face out there in the mountains.

As I think about the stresses, I wonder if I am the sort of person who has the stamina and the inner resolve to make a long walk. Fortunately, I know that many people much like me have successfully finished the AT. Most of them are much the better person for having done so. Reading their accounts gives me a feeling for the pleasures and the rigors of a long trail.

There are nurses and accountants and bricklayers and bums that have walked the whole AT. Big guys and little girls, oldsters and youngsters, and lots of people in between have started in Georgia and walked to Maine. A two hundred mile hike is shorter and easier.

Experience Preferred: There are very few major league pitchers who did not pitch in the minor leagues. The likelihood of success improves for athletes who have a strong record of experience. I pass a sign every day at a construction firm: "Hiring experienced construction workers." Every once in a while I wonder who hires the workers before they have experience so they can go out and get jobs. I wonder if it is that way for hikers too.

No one checks the credentials of hikers to see if they are qualified to start carrying a pack–no one except Mother Earth. She does her own checking up to see if the hiker is ready for rain and snow and cold and heat and hiking up large hills. And she is often not very gentle in vetting the hiker for ability and experience.

> *"If you take care of the little things, the big things are easy."*
> Shane Steinkamp
> (This quote and others from personal correspondence or the pages at www.theplacewithnoname.com. Shane is an accomplished long distance hiker and a friend.)

70 A Wildly Successful 200-Mile Hike

While it may be possible to successfully walk into an outfitter, buy equipment, show up at Springer and walk the whole AT with essentially no experience, the probability of success is not very high. I have spoken to people who start the trail that way every year I have been out there, and I have read their journals. Some of them finish in Maine, but not many. Most of them finish in Georgia.

I approach investments of my time very carefully–especially when it is vacation time. So early on when I began to get interested in long distance hiking I decided to *gradually* approach the idea of a thru-hike. I did not yet know if I was the sort of person who would enjoy hiking, or if I just liked the idea of thinking about hiking. But I knew one way to find out.

> *- I read/learned about hiking.*
> *- I talked about hiking.*
> *-Then, while the iron was hot, I went on a hike.*

First, I practiced in my yard. I learned how to sleep in a hammock when the temperature was below freezing. I learned how to cook food with a camp stove. I learned how to put everything in a pack, and then I did some day hiking with that pack on my back.

The first overnight hike was a 10-mile cool weather hike in March with my adult son, Daniel. The spot we chose was Zaleski State Park, a couple hours from my house in Ohio. I got to try out some of the ideas I had read about and had been trying in my yard experiments: trail shoes, hammock, tarp, hat, and stove. I loved every minute of it.

A couple months later I invested a week's worth of vacation time to sample the real thing–the Appalachian Trail.

It wasn't a long hike, but it was not a short one either. It was the longest hike I had ever taken–67 miles–and I discovered the AT was like no other trail I had ever walked. It was steeper, rockier, more slippery, and more beautiful than any hiking I had ever done. It was also an adventure in the company of other hikers (thru-hikers) dreaming of hiking the whole AT.

By then, I was head-over-heels in love with the idea and the experience of hiking the AT. But I did not have all the kinks worked out. There were equipment issues, pains, and some mental issues I needed to work out before taking on a really long hike. I had suffered from several days of quite severe knee pain, and also developed a big blister on one of my toes. I worked through the problems and took several more hikes that summer and fall. These progressively more difficult hikes set me up for the next step–a two-week vacation of hiking.

In May of 2004, I took the time to hike the 200-mile hike. That is where I am now, and the lessons learned on that hike are the substance of this bookl on successfully walking that distance–three times as far as I had ever previously hiked.

I am not satisfied with a 200-mile hike. But the next set of lessons learned will need to wait a year or two–until after I learn them!

I think there is great mental value in sneaking up on a long hike, as I have done. By the time I got to the trailhead of my 200-mile hike, I was at the next logical step in hiking. In the same way, the experience of a 200-mile hike makes a really long hike the next logical step.

However, there is a parallel path I have also explored. There is a way to get used to the idea of long distance hiking by reading about the experiences of others.

Armchair Hiking: I have long subscribed to a labor and knuckle-saving principle: My personal transcript does not need to list every course offered by the "School of Hard Knocks". Other graduates are regularly willing to share their lessons in such a way that I need not personally be admitted to the hospital, go hypothermic, or walk in exceeding pain.

They write about their experiences in books, magazine articles, and on the Internet. They talk about the problems they solved around the virtual campfire of meetings, talks, and list servers.

Books are an extremely valuable source of information. Two important genres predominate the bookshelves: how-to books, and trail journals. How-to books are great for learning what should be in my pack and how to use it. But, beyond them, for the business of getting mentally ready for the trail, I think the trail journals are worth every minute I've invested in reading their pages.

Here are a few books that I have learned important lessons from:

A Walk in the Woods by Bill Bryson: This is everyone's favorite book to hate or secretly love. Bryson helped me work through my fear of cold weather camping and persuaded me of the value of ultralight hiking. If Bryson and Katz could hike when the weather was below freezing, so could I.

Walkin' on the Happy Side of Misery by J.R. Tate: Oh the joy of an oooga! Model T has written a wonderfully funny book about everything from persuading a wife that walking the trail is a good idea, to unusual trail-born kitchen habits, to the importance of friendships built on the trail. This is a great book to help understand how different hiking styles lead hiking partners to begin hiking more quickly or slowly and what it is like for friends to lose touch with one another on a long hike.

The Appalachian Trail–A Journey of Discovery by Jan D. Curran: His story is about what it is like for a 50 year old military retiree to tackle the trail and deal with recurrent health problems. His introspection is never as detailed as the wonderful description of characters he meets on the trail, but the account is a great way to see the trail from the eyes of a military retiree like me. The variety of good and bad days, and how Jan deals with them, helps me to get an important understanding of the trail experience

As Far as the Eye Can See by David Brill: Brill's book is well written prose bordering on poetic. The book is about the trail 25 years ago, but the woods don't change much. Thunderstorms still rock through the southern passes and unusual characters still walk the trail. This book helped me become more aware of my spiritual experience and has given me more appreciation for my thoughts while actually hiking on the AT.

Walking with Spring by Earl Shaffer: The absolute classic book about the trail by its first thru-hiker is still a great read. The trail has changed since 1948, but much of the emotional experience of a young man facing the trail absolutely alone still courses through my own veins, even with the passage of years and the increased popularity of the AT.

These books are good reading before a long hike, during the hike, and afterward. Not everything that I needed to learn about hiking can be learned by reading. Real on-the-trail experience cannot be replaced. This is especially true when learning about how I will respond to various stresses, especially since each individual responds in a unique way to stresses.

Stress Gauge: The psychiatrists say that stress is a good thing and a bad thing. It depends. (How does that make you feel?) Stress can promote growth and cause strengths to emerge. But stress can also overwhelm me when I come upon a junction of many stresses simultaneously.

My friend quips that I make too much of a deal about the idea of stress while hiking:

> *"What stress? You're walking around looking at pretty scenery all day, eating snacks, sleeping whenever you want to.... I just don't buy the stress angle. When I'm in the wilderness is the only time that I feel like everything is going to be OK. It's the only place I feel safe. Darkness and loneliness are my dearest friends. My danger isn't going home early, my danger is never going home...because I am home...."*
> -Shane Steinkamp

But, while I identify with the concept of the forest as one of my homes, I do feel some stress in the woods.

Some of my mental stress while hiking 200 miles is coupled to physical deprivation and pain. Others parts of the stress burden are linked to loss or change. Stresses that include pain, cold, heat, friction, or wetness can result in physical injury or illness. Stresses whose root cause is loss can degenerate into moodiness, loss of a sense of humor, and depression.

76 A Wildly Successful 200-Mile Hike

Here are some stresses I have observed and some of my defenses against letting them wear me down to injury or depression:

Being alone: Fortunately, I like myself. I like to listen to myself talk. I like the music I play, and the ideas I have, and the pictures I take. I like to pray and whittle and cook. I absolutely adore the idea of walking, by myself, for a full day and spending a total of 5 minutes talking along the way. I like to think about how I will share what I have seen and what I have thought. But I seldom have a desire for others to be with me, seeing it with me.

Not everyone feels this way. My wife wishes constantly that our children or other extended family were here, right now. She pines for them to be with her, hearing the falls, seeing the deer, watching the leaves swirl in the wind. We joke each time she spontaneously says "Wouldn't it be wonderful if (mother / son / daughter / friend) were here. We need to get them out here. It is so beautiful." It is not so much a wishing they were seeing the splendor of nature, as it is a desire that they experience it with her. She combats the stress of being alone by arranging to be with me, or her friends, or our kids or someone she meets on the trail. Avoiding being alone is certainly a valid defense against the stress of being alone.

Fortunately, the AT allows either preference. I can be alone, by myself. But the trail also gives the opportunity of being with a group if that is what gives pleasure.

But learning how to be adaptable also is useful. When I happen to not be alone, I enjoy the time with my companions. When she is on her own, she remembers that aloneness never lasts forever and that she will enjoy the renewed company of fellow hikers even more.

Loneliness: Distinct from "being alone" as a stress, loneliness is experienced as dejection or melancholy resulting from an awareness of being separated. There are people who enjoy being alone, but I have never found a person who enjoys loneliness.

Loneliness–or rather its avoidance–is one of the fuels of love. It may already be obvious that any stress that can drive a young man or woman to marriage can be powerful enough to drive them off the trail.

I have been hungry without a second-by-second awareness of the emptiness in my stomach. I have also been hungry enough that every moment without food is an intolerable burden. Loneliness is related to that gnawing emptiness. It is a craving for companionship with a specific person–especially family.

While loneliness may be a large stress in a multi-month hike, it is less likely to cause failure of a 2- or 3-week-long 200-mile hike.

Much of the loneliness stress can be handled with telephone calls and keeping in touch. Pay phones are available in trail towns and can be found every few days on a 200-mile hike. Keeping up by email is also possible using Web email systems and Internet terminals in town libraries.

Another way to avoid the stress of loneliness is to prepare all house payments, bills, responses to invitations, and other personal business before heading out on the trail. Sharing loving moments during the occasional telephone calls instead of arranging personal business makes such calls better for both the hiker and those who are still at the homestead.

The Fun Meter is Pegged (sigh): Even when I am successful dealing with loneliness, the excitement of hiking long days does not last forever. I occasionally get bored with the hike.

Sometimes the whole hike just does not seem all that interesting. "Been there, done that" comes to mind when another foggy day keeps me from seeing sights or one more day of rain proves that my shoes are not as waterproof as I believed they were.

> *"It isn't the mountain that wears you down. It's the rock in your shoe."*
> *-Unknown writer*

It's not always the big things, sometimes it is the little ones that begin to grate.

Losing the Will to Hike

A term learned from other hikers early in my journey was the always-dreaded PUD. "Pointless Ups and Downs" are seen by exhausted footsloggers as the mischievous work of trail workers to force 1000 foot climbs up and down mountainsides for no apparent reason. In essence, thinking about a wooded mountain as a PUD is evidence of the loss of the joy of hiking and a manifestation of boredom.

I only know one way to combat boredom in hiking–staying excited, the process of keeping the "fun meter" pegged all the way to the right. The way I keep having fun is by actively playing. Some forms of this play are listed here:

> *- Staying aware of where I am and when I will arrive at the next point on the trail. How many miles per hour am I walking?*
>
> *- Singing in rhythm to my walking, making up verses to familiar tunes, whistling songs I knew ages ago*
>
> *- Thinking of ways to improve part of my hiking gear*
>
> *- Talking or telling a story to a fellow hiker*
>
> *- Seeing how many birds I can identify from their calls or by sight–how many*

> trees I know in this woods—what edible plants are to be found
>
> - Writing a character sketch or description of some part of the trail for my journal
>
> - Taking a skinny dipping bath in a stream, swimming, running through a field, taking an undeserved nap
>
> - Drying my socks, tarp, or clothes in a sunny clearing

Activities like these, and anything else that comes to mind during a trip, keep me fresh and have the advantage of not leaving enough time to get bored.

Rain, Rain, Go Away: An old thru-hiker figured out that it rains 1/3 of the days on the trail. It is hot and unbearable 1/3 of the time. Cold, snow, or fog dominates 1/3 of the solar cycles. The rest of the time is just perfect.

It is an unresolved mystery why most people love to swim or bathe, and why the same people seldom enjoy walking in the rain. But finding a person who likes walking in the rain is as common as finding a stone arrowhead. It is common for hikers to hurry to a shelter to avoid a rainstorm, and to delay leaving in the morning while any hope holds for rain to cease.

The way I deal with the stress of weather is to learn to be comfortable regardless of the situation. My goal is to know enough and to apply it well, so that weather is a fact and not a worry. The better I get at comfortably walking in the rain for hours on end, the more I feel kinship with all creatures of the forest. The more skill I develop at remaining dry and warm while sleeping in the rain, the more I feel at home in the mountains.

I used to be concerned about weather all the time. I wanted to have a weather radio and know what the temperature was going to be in 12 hours. It was, I guess, just to have sufficient time to adequately worry about the weather. The more I hike, the more I realize that I am pretty awful (as are the weather forecasters) at guessing what the weather will be like in 12 hours. But I am really good at telling what the weather is right now! I can perceive if it is raining or snowing or windy or hot or dry with the best of them.

My goal is to be as unworried about standing and walking in the rain (or sun or cold or heat) as a deer or a cardinal. What I have developed is the ability to respond to changes in the weather in less than 30 seconds. I can deploy my protection from rain, either on the trail or in camp, very quickly.

Making a measured response is also part of my bag of tricks. I have learned to tie a tarp over my hammock but to leave it in its "sausage tube" cover unless/until it is needed. That way, if it starts looking like rain or starts sprinkling in the middle of the night, I can have the four corners of the tarp pegged in a few seconds.

I wear a rainproof hat all the time; so a little sprinkle during the day causes me no worry. I can put a rain cover on my pack that doubles as a covering for my torso in a few seconds. I can add leggings or arm covers to that central core in a few more moments.

A simple summary of the way I deal with weather stress is to eliminate the worry. Quite literally, I strive to be a man for all seasons. Regardless of how unexpected a weather change might be, I am already prepared. I have a very different strategy to deal with the next stress.

They All Go Marching Down to the Ground: Pace and fatigue are intimately related in my mind for most of the time I am walking in the backcountry. The better the pace I keep up, the more fatigued I become. The more I cater to provisions to reduce fatigue, the more my pace and daily mileage drop off.

I really do like walking and getting down the trail. However I do not like to walk quickly. As I begin a day's walk, I have a goal in mind for my stopping point, and even for two general areas for lunch breaks. However, I always remain flexible as those plans work out. Sometimes an expected view is nothing but a wind-swept foggy rock. Other times an entrancing vista emerges. I expect that somewhere during the day I will find a spot that emits an atmosphere of fascination. I don't know if it will be a cliff, a fire tower, a flower, or a shelter full of boy scouts having lunch.

I have learned it is a poor idea for me to plan on a "death march" to reach a spot on the trail which will exhaust me. On very few occasions I have pushed myself to mileage goals for the day which were quite exhausting. For instance, my walking more than 12 hours seems to be a bad idea.

What were the causes of the worst of my hyper-treks? One was caused by pure ignorance–it was my first section hike on the AT and I had figured I could walk for 16 hours a day like Ray Jardine. It turns out that I am not like Ray Jardine (big surprise).

The other times I have extended a hiking day beyond my ability it was to shorten a hike by a day and get home. One such day was a cool and windy walk in the Smoky Mountains. I looked at the hiking in front of me and decided I had the time to stretch an 18-mile day into a 24-mile day. It was near the end of my 200-mile hike and it would give me the opportunity to get home a day earlier after being gone for two weeks.

I was tired and standing next to a shelter at the 18-mile point, but I doggedly moved on. The next six miles were exhausting and I walked into the shelter late in the evening, just before a storm. During the last few miles, my sense of humor was not in high gear. Even worse, I only remember that part of the trail as being tiring. The beautiful views were just a place to sit for a moment and try to decide if I was going to have time to make it to the shelter before I collapsed from exhaustion.

I find it much better to walk until I have spent a day's walking and even want to walk a little further. It is always better for me to want more than I get, than to get more than I want.

When I am hammock camping, I can decide to stop almost anywhere there are trees and have camp set up in twenty minutes. There is a big advantage of not needing to find a flat place for a tent when fatigue sets in. Being freed from the restrictions of shelter or tent site geography reduces my mental stress from fear of getting so fatigued I cannot continue.

It also helps me to remember to enjoy each mile. I am not out in the woods to set a speed record, compete with other hikers, or to make it home for Christmas. I am walking instead of driving to have fun seeing everything. Rushing is a stress I know I don't have to apply to myself.

Sleep, Deep Sleep: Getting a good night's sleep is very important in maintaining the will to hike. Hiking is moderate exercise multiplied times many hours of a walking day. The exhaustion of a day on the trail is often enough to get me to sleep, but staying asleep is sometimes not so easy. Rocks and roots can become tiresome bedfellows for tent campers. When I stay in a shelter, the snoring of my fellow hikers and the scampering of mice can wake me and keep me awake.

This is one reason I really enjoy hammock sleeping. I am almost always able to hang far enough away from the crowd that I hear no snoring. Mice do not bother me this far away from a shelter. And I have the same wonderful sleeping surface night after night, with never a root or a rock poking my tender skin. In the morning, I almost always am able to wake refreshed, recharged, and ready for whatever the trail has down its way for me to discover.

Sometimes, the sleep is interrupted by vivid dreams. Occasionally, I may need to get up and walk around a bit to get my mind on something else. But there are nightmares that are really crippling.

What Goes Bump in the Night: In a long conversation with a hiking friend that extended over a two-day period, I learned that he had stopped a thru-hike entirely because of a dramatic nightmare on the trail. It went something like this:

> *After three long and exhausting days on the trail, John had arrived at Betty Creek Gap on the AT. He had laid up in Hiwassee to get rid of a case of bronchitis which had plagued him since he started at Springer. This was his third*

day back on the trail.

Betty Creek Gap is about 70 miles north of Springer Mountain. The day had been long, and John had not had much sleep for days and days.

There was a suitable tenting spot among the rhododendron bushes and trees just to the right of the trail. He set up his tarp and crawled into his sleeping bag to take a nap about 3 PM. He had barely unpacked anything in his pack and it was several yards away from the tarp.

He awoke with a start sometime in the middle of the night after having a disturbing nightmare. (Nightmares or very vivid dreams are common when sleep has been interrupted for a number of preceding nights. The need to dream is universal.) His heart was racing and he felt quite closed in. It was also difficult to comprehend why it had suddenly turned so dark—hadn't he just laid down for a nap?

John had lost his flashlight the day before at Standing Indian shelter. He did have a stove that could throw some light, but it was in his pack, completely out of reach. The night was that kind of moonless, cloudy night that is particularly dark, and was even more so under the thick canopy of trees. He could not see his hand in front of his face.

In fact, getting his hand up to his face was a problem. The sleeping bag was zipped up and tight enough that he could not easily sneak a hand up to the opening.

He also could not see where the zipper pull for the sleeping bag was.

It was a nice March morning when John was telling me the story. But the hair on the back of my neck was beginning to stand erect. In that inky blackness, John freaked out. He strained to reach where he thought the zipper for the bag was as the adrenalin from the nerve-wracking dream still coursed through his veins. The sleeping bag zipper kept jamming as he tried to open it in the dark. Finally, with the sleeping bag open far enough to wiggle out, he was able to grope his way out of the tarp and start trying to find his pack.

Minutes later, he finally found the pack in the darkness. He felt for the stove and some matches. As the glow from the stove lit up his world, his mental world began to come back into focus.

> *John told me that he laid back down, but that the claustrophobic feeling returned. He fought it and stayed in the sleeping bag. But somewhere in those dark morning hours, he decided that he had had enough. He was going to leave the trail. He was not going to spend another night in that tent.*
>
> *He did leave the trail. He also spent the next 6 months unable to let himself get shut up in an airplane or a small room. It was disabling.*

Other stories have been just as real, but not as dramatic. I distinctly remember a hiker in the Smoky Mountains named Hawk who was very quiet all evening in the shelter. However, somewhere in the darkness of the night, a gang apparently surrounded him in his dream. The language he used when he was loudly yelling at the gang members was as dramatic as it was coarse. It took us all a little while to fall back asleep after that episode.

Dreams can be expected to sometimes be vivid and even frightening. As I mentioned before, getting good sleep is sometimes difficult outdoors. Several days of interrupted sleep can result in a violent or otherwise fear-provoking set of dreams on a later night. It is worth remembering that such frightening dreams are not a sign of mental instability or the inability to keep hiking. Sharing the dream with a trail friend is sometimes a good way to dilute the overwhelming emotional response to the dream.

OK, So Those are the Stresses, What Can I Do About It? The resources available to the hiker are all around, as well as inside. Sometimes it takes some searching to find them, but we have within ourselves the ability to deal with most stresses the trail can throw our way.

Stress, like beauty, depends on the experience of the beholder. There are some experiences which are beautiful to a large majority of people and there are also a set of stresses which are bothersome to nearly everyone. In a similar way, what works to make stress manageable for one person might not work for everyone, but what works for many people is likely to be helpful.

The OOOH...AHHH...Factor: A deep appreciation of the wonder of creation is a frequent source of the strength I need in the face of stress. Hiking allows me views of nature not achieved in any other way. A list and description of the beautiful things I see in a single trail day could fill a book this size several times over.

Sometimes the beauty is classic postcard stuff–lakes and cliffs and valleys under a bright blue sky. Other times it is the shape of a bright orange fungus growing on a dead pine. Or it might be bleached trunks of a ghost forest of firs in a dense fog.

I try to look around me with appreciation whenever I sit and rest. Sometimes I look at the view in front of me, and sometimes I take time to notice the insects and spiders whose home I have chosen to sit on.

Whenever I take the time to really look around me at the beauty and complexity of creation and then come back to the stress that was just burdening me, it helps me to refocus the center of my attention. Then, I am able to understand from a fresh perspective that the problem causing me stress is not as overwhelming as it seemed a few minutes ago. What's more, a new solution frequently bubbles to the surface. The solution may be related to the natural creation's way of dealing with the stress, or may just be a fresh idea unleashed from my mind when I was thinking of something besides myself.

An example is the use of sassafras cuttings in my hat to ward off mosquitoes and other insects. One afternoon I was struggling to retain my cool. I sat down to think about how other animals might deal with the bugs. A picture of a cow swishing her tail across her back to be rid of biting flies came to mind. That reminded me of Earl Schaffer's solution for insects. He had used cuttings of Sassafras against the insects. I cut a few leaves the next time I saw a sassafras tree, stuck them in my hat band, and it worked to keep the bugs at bay.

Learning is Fun: I deeply believe that understanding something for the first time is the most treasured of human experiences. It separates us from all other living creatures. Understanding is more than a conditioned reflex or an expectation of reward. It encompasses a situation, including the emotion, actions and characters, the intellectual relationships, and a mind-model of what is actually going on in reality.

While all learning is fun, it does not always *seem* to be fun. Certainly, the *process* of learning (homework, tests, school) is not always fun. But, the *accomplished act* of learning is worthwhile on a deep level

As an adult, stresses are the best opportunity I have to learn something new. Stress is also the opportunity to apply spiritual strength developed over a lifetime of taking the time to observe, learn and grow.

Hiking almost always presents multiple opportunities to learn every day. Some of the best learning is about the natural world around me. It is fascinating to observe the interpersonal relationships of hikers in a novel human situation, trail life. But not every learning opportunity is pleasant.

Whenever I come face to face with the panting and pawing beast of a dilemma, I take a moment to gather spiritual strength of past victories–mine, the conquests of friends, and even those of the ancestors of people who lived in the Appalachian Mountains for countless generations.

Lessons from Native Americans: When facing a stress, I often hearken back to the ethics of people who lived on this continent before the 16th century arrival of Europeans.

The Sioux nation probably never lived in the high mountains of the East Coast. Their culture was described in detail by historians who left contemporary written records in the 19th century. As I have read of the Sioux cultural traditions, the sense of living in the forest as home instead of wilderness rings resonant with my hiking experience.

Among the ethics of the Lakota Sioux, bravery and perseverance ranked among the highest virtues, And I have found success in applying the moral values of bravery and perseverance. Bravery gives me the strength to stand in the face of overwhelming adversity without cowering in fear. It gives me the ability to act instead of falling apart. Perseverance follows up on the heels of bravery with a constant strength in the face of cold, pain, loneliness, or frightening circumstance.

When bravery is called for, nothing else will do. One specific morning comes to mind, while I was crossing the grassy tops of the Roan Highlands south from the Overmountain Shelter in the aftermath of a giant east coast hurricane. Winds were sustained above 40 mph and gusting to 60. The winds carried fog and pelting rain. The worst of the gusts pushed me completely off the path despite leaning against the wind between gusts. The rain was between 40 and 50 degrees. I had never walked in weather as extreme. I knew that I could follow the deep pathway through the meadows and not become lost, but it still took all the personal energy I had to walk through that cold/wet day without complaining or becoming discouraged. I did not know how much energy I was putting into the effort until I reached a group of pine trees above Carver's Gap and breathed an audible sigh of relief at finally being across the wind swept mountain top.

Perseverance is nothing more than the decision that continuing is better than stopping and giving up. An example from my canoe camping background comes to mind. Long ago, my sister and I were bucking a heavy wind on a Boundary Waters lake in Minnesota. We were making slow but frustrating progress against the wind. It seemed like we would make progress for a couple strokes and then be driven backward during the third stroke. After a half hour of this strain, 15 year-old Lisa finally threw her paddle down in disgust saying that she could do no more. I calmly kept paddling like only a cocky 17-year old brother can, and told her that if she could not paddle, then she could not, and not to worry about it. After a couple minutes of waiting for me to give up, she picked up her paddle and began to pull into the wind again. Perseverance is picking the paddle back up.

When I think of examples of perseverance, I remember those days walking with bone grinding knee pain south of Erwin and nearly the whole trip from Clingman's Dome to Hot Springs, where my problem was an irritated (and it turns out infected) blister on the back of my left heel.

On a Wing and a Prayer: Belief in a loving God also gives me refreshment in dark times. I pray whenever it suits the occasion, and I like to stay in the habit of praying. I enjoy the great views with God and the worst pains. It certainly beats talking to myself. God the Father is an infinite resource for strength, wisdom, composure, and forgiveness. It is reassuring to know that even when I don't love me, God does. And there are times when that is important.

Because my family members share my belief, I am supported by their prayers, too. In an earlier chapter I shared how a conversation with my wife led to discovery of the short step technique going downhill to preserve and even treat knee pain. That discovery came immediately after a cell phone conversation with Diane, and very shortly after she prayed for me. The technique was one I had never read or heard about, though I am certainly not the first to discover it. It was, I am convinced, the direct intervention of God the Father to help me keep walking in his woods.

Preventing "Brain Rot":

There are two additional tools I carry in my hip pocket to deal with the mental stresses of hiking. Both are classic preventive medicine approaches.

I think of them as my immunization shots for "brain rot." The first is a story, and the second is a plan.

The number of people who ask about a hike not yet taken is honestly incredible. (The opposite is true about the number of people who want to hear about the hike once it is complete.) So, I find it helpful to learn how to tell "the hike story" well. I have versions for the person who wants a ten-second quote, for the person who has a minute, and for the serious seeker who wants to talk for an hour. The story always involves goals. Knowing my hiking goals helps me to hop from one mountaintop to the next when sodden days of walking in muck may lie between. So I use all those opportunities when people ask me why I am hiking to re-immunize my brain from the effects of stress.

My personal goals in almost any hike are:

> - to enjoy what non-hikers never get the chance to see
> - to learn more about myself both mentally and physically
> - to learn more about a lightweight lifestyle
> - to gather new material for new stories.

From this, the ten-second answer to the questioner is some variation of, "I really enjoy seeing the country at the speed of a stroll, and to stop where and when I feel like it."

The other important tool I take with me every day is a deliberate plan for how I will leave the trail if I need to do so before I reach my goal. I credit long-distance hiker "PapaJohn" Kennedy for the idea of this preventative. We brainstormed some of the items together when hiking Albert Mountain in the spring of 2004.

Simply put, I put certain restrictions on any decision I make to quit the trail prematurely:

- *I will not make this decision by myself.*
- *I will talk it over with a friend face-to-face.*
- *I will talk it over with my wife.*
- *I will not decide to leave at night or when it is raining.*
- *If I decide to leave, I will leave myself a viable alternative to stay on the trail two days hence. (I will not ask anyone to come pick me up until I have had two days to think it through a thousand times.)*
- *If I leave, I will never complain about my hike, the people I was with, or the weather. I only get to do that if I complete the hike.*

- *If I leave, I will give myself opportu-*

nity to return to the trail two weeks later, no questions asked.

This second tool, the "leave the trail plan," can be very effective in dealing with most trail stresses. Like the old saw says, a perfect day will be coming up any day now. It is a better idea to make the decision to leave the trail when all is well than when life is like "hell in a hand basket."

Know Myself: Beyond tools, prevention, book learning, and philosophy, one of the greatest resources that keeps me on the trail during good times and hard times is actually developed on the trail.

It's me.

And it is my understanding of me.

I've done work already in life to understand myself. But every novel situation, after I have had time to reflect on it, leads to more understanding. It may be a new story, or a feeling finally understood, or a primal response to the woods as home. But every time I go out hiking I find out more about myself.

I am in the continuous process of developing a philosophy of hiking. I know that my goal is to travel lightly and by foot, to see what I have missed my whole life because cars are too fast and aircraft too high.

98 A Wildly Successful 200-Mile Hike

I realize it is important to me to know that I made most of what I carry, and that I have given thought to its impact on the environment and my fellow hikers.

Beyond my personal philosophy, I have learned a great deal about the benefit of attitudes that fit trail life on the AT. This next section conveys a number of these attitudes, paraphrased from various sources.

>   -Having fun. Learn!
>   -Tolerance. Both for healthy discomfort, and others behavior
>   -Self Awareness. Ability to recognize my own mental state and be able to adjust for it
>   -Self Control. Acting in a different way than my first impulse when that is harmful
>   -Flexibility. Ready to change my plans when they fall apart
>   -Risk Taking. Can I correctly diagnose risks as adventure (Do it!) versus danger (No way!)?
>   -Innovation. Creative problem solving by combining bits of knowledge
>   -Stopping early. Know my limits and quit while I'm ahead
>   -Relax. Even when things go bad, relaxing is better than panic
>   -Plan the end game. Always have backup and bailout plans

Doctorate in Hiking Program: Shane Steinkamp and I have entered into a long dialog about why people hike. There are certainly many reasons people give for their hiking. However, Shane asserts that there is one reason that all hikers share.

> *The Grand Unification Theory says that everybody hikes, camps, and enters the outdoors for the same reason, the ultimate reason. That reason is to reconnect as natural animals in and with our natural habitat. This isn't something you necessarily work for; it's just something that happens to you one day...*

I have not observed this to be generally true of everyone who walks a trail. However, the words match well with the primitive kinship I feel for the time I spend hiking in the outdoors.

There was a time when I felt like an explorer while I was hiking. I needed to be prepared for this dangerous place I was entering. If I prepared well, then perhaps I would emerge at the end of the adventure unharmed by the experience. It was a little like the decision to throw myself out the door of an airplane so that I could parachute safely to the earth.

Over time, this feeling of the wilderness as a wild place has been replaced by the acceptance of the forest as a place which offers comfort and nurture.

I am more than an animal in the woods. I am a spiritual being able to experience the outdoors in ways too deep for other creatures to appreciate. However, I am also able to experience the feeling of home that forest animals feel. This is because while I am hiking, I am a forest creature.

* * *

This chapter has explored the many reasons that can cause me to lose the will to hike. Among the major stresses are lack of experience, lack of knowledge, physical stress, loneliness, boredom, weather, fatigue, and lack of rest.

Tools that help me stay on the trail include appreciating the natural wonder, bravery, perseverance, prayer, and a clear set of goals.

Overall, the book has covered three major problems on the trail, the bedfellows of friction, knee problems, and the dynamics in a hiker's mind.

In the next chapter, I move away from problems found on a 200-mile hike, to concentrate on one best technique. It is a partial solution to many of the problems. It almost makes them vanish into thin air.

Chapter 5

The One Best Idea

A 15 pound pack: This chapter is a catalyst that goes above and beyond the examination of the Three Biggest Problems (friction – knees – mental will). Instead of describing a problem it is a description of a solution. These pages describe in depth the one best idea I have worked with in hiking the Appalachian Trail–a lightweight pack.

Not Again! Once more I have forgotten to take my pack off during an hourly rest break. I have been sitting here, resting my feet for the last five minutes, oblivious to the pack on my back. How could I sit here resting and forget to take my pack off!

It has not always been this way. When I backpacked as a boy scout, many of my memories are of the unremitting pain of carrying a backpack. The bones, muscles and skin of my shoulders hurt. The skin of my back and hips also hurt as the pack rubbed those areas raw.

Stopping for a rest with a heavy pack always meant searching for a special place. I remember looking around desperately for a place to support the weight of my pack while it was still on my back. Sometimes I could find a rock or a fallen tree that would temporarily hold the weight so I did not have to swing the 50-pound pack from my back another time.

Moving forward 35 years, my pack has now gotten light enough that the weight of the pack pressing on my muscles and bones is no longer the center of my thinking. Just the opposite–almost forget the pack is there. It is not because I am stronger at age fifty-two than I was at seventeen. It is not really because camping equipment has improved in some dramatic way. It is because I have *decided* to carry no more than a lightweight pack.

Backpacking is No Longer about the Backpack: I don't go out into the woods to carry a backpack. I go out to hike and have fun and learn. I'd much rather call it hiking than packing. One of the tools I use is a backpack. It is full of what I need to stay out in the woods in any weather for a while.

So, what is magical about a 15-pound pack? Why is it the "one best idea?" For me, it is the maximum weight I can carry and forget it is on my back. Maybe for another hiker the "Forget It" pack weight is a little higher or lower. For me it is just about 15 pounds.

I have read many of Internet postings by people who try to come up with the absolutely lightest pack–lighter than everyone else has carried. I don't put much credence in this competitive ultralight pack comparison, though pack lists like this may give me some ideas to think about for my own pack. It is not important to me to have the lightest pack. "Forget It" weight is good enough.

Here are some tests to see if I am still in the "Forget It" weight class:

- When I take my pack off, do I easily swing it from my shoulders with one hand?
- If someone offers to drive my pack to a road crossing (slack pack a section) does the offer sound amusing?
- Do I sometimes forget to take my pack off when resting?
- When stopping to talk for a few minutes on the trail, do I leave my pack on solely because I forgot to take it off?
- When walking down a side trail to a spring, does it seem strange to leave the pack at the trail intersection instead of carrying it to the spring?

I do believe there is such a thing as a too-light pack. If I need to borrow something on the trail once a week, I did not pack what I needed. If I need to borrow something to survive, it was a dumb decision to leave that thing at home.

What do I carry? To begin with, I need and carry anything I use every day. Only maybe do I need to carry something I use once a week. But, almost everything which stays in my pack unused, should not have been in the pack to begin with. (A few emergency supplies may be an exception. For me, that means a sewing kit and some duct tape.)

The list of things that I actually need is shorter than the list of things I used to carry on the trail. Like most hikers, I used to carry far too much, which weighed way too much, and was too bulky.

Parallel example from canoe camping: A few years ago, my son and I carried a total of about 130 pounds of gear plus a canoe, when we camped in the Boundary Waters Canoe Area. We had three Duluth Bags crammed full of gear, and a daypack besides. This was for a 5-day trip. By applying some of the lessons learned from AT thru-hikers we easily trimmed our load down to about 25 pounds apiece in two years of effort. And that weight included several pounds of fishing gear. We needed three trips to cross a portage between lakes that first year. By the last year, we could cross a mile long portage without stopping to rest, and we could do it with all our gear in one trip.

So what does this canoe example mean for a 200-mile hike? Well, one limit has been found. I know how to pack too much. I am still searching for the other limit–packing not enough. I know it exists, but I have not quite found it yet. I know the lower bound would be reached if I found that I was missing something I needed to have fun every day. I know the lower bound would have been crossed if I needed to borrow equipment, a place to sleep, or food for conditions I should have expected.

What I do know is that I have gotten to the point where I frequently forget about my pack. Trimming pack weight below this "Forget It" limit has minimal gain in making my hiking more successful, and risks encountering a situation where I need to borrow equipment to hike my hike.

Method for Packing a 15-Pound Pack: After reading several ultralight philosophers, I have boiled down the collected wisdom into two triplets of thought:

- *Be prepared for what will happen*
- *Don't be prepared for what will not happen*
- *Be prepared to improvise*

- *Take what is needed*
- *Leave behind what is not needed*
- *Adapt to unusual stress*

- *Packing light begins with thinking light*
- *Thinking light requires an end to fear*
- *Hiking without fear makes a light pack*

I've given some thought as to whether I have a system for what I carry in my lightweight pack. I've concluded that since everything works together in the end, it is a system. But it is not a religious covenant to adhere to a hiking system.

I really dislike the idea of patterning pack lists and choices after well-known authors. Adhering like groupies to the experience of these well-known hikers, several competing schools of ultralight hiking have developed. That's not for me, though each may have some practices I have adopted.

I tweak my system all the time. I am not afraid of breaking the system by trying something new. I just think through how it might affect everything else and then try it out. I try to use any new gear in a fairly safe environment first, and then take it further and further into the wilderness.

What I actually do: I decided to live a lightweight lifestyle. I decided to enjoy where I am more than what I carry. I decided to live frugally and simply.

I decided to learn best practices for a lightweight pack from all available sources. I began by reading Ray Jardine's "Beyond Backpacking," but have read much good information on the Internet as well. In addition, I paid attention to what other experienced hikers are carrying.

I care about how much everything weighs, individually and collectively. If something is lighter and works, it is better, period. I pay attention to what I actually use. I stop carrying things I don't use daily unless the need to carry them is necessary to avoid reasonably probable life-threatening risk. I pay attention to the opportunity to make it all work together in a systematic way. For example, I ask, "How light does all this stuff need to be before I can downsize from a seven-pound pack to a three-pound one and then to a half-pound one? "

I carry much less clothing than I ever believed possible. The only thing I carry two of is pairs of socks. That's because I frequently use two pairs in a day. The shirt on my back is my only shirt. I wash it near a stream and put it back on to dry. My swimsuit is the only pair of shorts or underwear I carry. My kilt/skirt is the only long garment I have. My rain jacket is my only jacket.

I don't take things I don't use. Sunglasses proved useless on the long woodland trail we call the AT. A compass was never needed–directions can usually be deduced from the position of the sun in the sky and the white blazes. There is nothing to shoot so I don't take a gun. I don't take time to fish. I don't play board games on the trail–I tell stories instead.

I do take some toys to play with (camera, Native American flute, journal, paperback book, cell phone), but I try to keep all of it as lightweight as possible.

I am very careful to pack the lightest food I need and I eat it all. I experiment with all sorts of dry food in the grocery store and find food that is as tasty to me as it is lightweight and full of calories and protein. I try to carry no water in any food. I take a multivitamin each day because I assume weight constraints will make it unlikely for me to have a balanced diet. The goal for the weight of my food is about 1.5 pounds of food a day.

Since carbohydrates give about 5 calories per gram and fats are about 9 calories per gram, I'd really like to aim at about 6 calories per gram in the food I carry. 680 grams (about a pound and a half) of food can theoretically yield about 4100 calories. However, with the fluff and some packaging in food that cannot be digested, about the best I actually do is about 3000 calories in my daily food allotment. That is plenty for a 200-mile hike.

It's really not hard or technical to put together the food list. My typical daily diet is two pop-tarts, a cup and a half of trail mix, a package of noodles and a few pieces of beef jerky. I looked all the calories up once, and now know approximately what I will need.

When the hike stretches to 800-2000 miles I know I will need to increase my daily calorie average to 4000-5000 calories per day if I am going to stop losing weight.

If I have decided to carry something, I obtain the lightest and highest quality version I can possibly afford. This frequently means sewing and building equipment for myself. Too often, commercial equipment is over-engineered or of poor quality.

Fear Factor: It is easy to let "fears of what might be" empty my wallet, add useless weight to my pack, and ruin a hike. More than anything else, reducing weight in my pack has been a process of leaving fears behind. It has turned out to be a rational process and not an unreasonable application of optimism. I still prepare for rain, I just don't need 6 sets of clothes to get through the rain.

The Big Four: I pay attention to the "Big Four" items in my pack, and work hard to increase their value by decreasing their weight. This "Big Four" includes the shelter, cook gear, sleeping bag, and pack.

After a good deal of experimenting, I have decided to carry a very lightweight camping hammock system including insulation and a tarp. It is the lightest weight sleeping arrangement I have found that works most places on the AT. Unlike a tarp-tent, it requires very little pad weight to make a comfortable bed to sleep all night and wake full of energy. Also, there is almost always a place to hang a hammock, while finding a somewhat flat spot for a ground sleeping system is often difficult. The weight of my hammock and tarp comes in right at two pounds.

For my cooking, I either use an alcohol stove or a twig stove. Commercial versions of twig stoves are all too heavy, so I make my own. Alcohol stoves can bought or homemade. Several homemade stoves are quite efficient. I carry a three-cup pot with a cozy to wrap around it so that I can cook noodle dishes after the fire has gone out. My goal for a complete cook system including flatware, bowl/pot, stove, and matches is under a half pound.

Because a quilt works better in a hammock for me than a sleeping bag, I have made a 1.5-pound down quilt.

Because I always keep my pack weight under twenty pounds, I am able to use a half-pound pack without a hip belt.

> *My Big Four weighs:*
> 2.0 lb   Hammock System
> 0.5   Cooking system
> 1.5   Quilt
> 0.5   Pack
>
> *Food for 5 days at 1.5 pounds per day:*
> 7.5 lb   Food
>
> *Clothing carried, (including rain gear)*
> 3.0 lb   Extra Clothes
> 15 lb   Total

That leaves nothing for "toys" of various sorts.

Unfortunately, I have about two or three pounds of toys which I really do use every day and which make my walk much more fun. So I average out the food weight (I carry only half of it on the average day) and call it 4 pounds. That brings the total to 11.5 pounds, and I get to carry up to 3 and a half pounds of my toys.

Sometimes it helps to have a checklist of things to take out of my pack. Here is one:

> - *Anything I walked out of an outfitter store with that I did not plan to get when I entered the store*
> - *Anything I think I might need, but*

*have not thought it through
- Anything that is more than 20 percent water weight
- Anything that is in style
- Anything made of steel
- Anything clothing made of cotton*

* * *

Being able to carry a "Forget It" weight pack is the most important personal discovery about hiking I have made in the last five years. Getting pack weight down involves a rational approach to what gear actually gets used, more than anything else. I have had to abandon irrational fears of what might happen and concentrate on what actually does happen when I am hiking.

Having the lightest pack wins no awards or even bragging rights. It is not nearly as respected as being either self sufficient (or cheerful) in the trail community. The reason to keep pack weight down is to be able to *walk well*. I'll cover that and tie up a few loose ends in the next chapter which is quite reasonably titled...

112 A Wildly Successful 200-Mile Hike

Chapter 6

The End of the Beginning

> *Now this is not the end. It is not even the beginning of the end. But it is, perhaps, the end of the beginning.*
>
> *Winston Churchill*
> *November 10, 1942*

Loose Ends? There are a few ideas in this book which need to be tied up. Inevitably, by dividing the problems and ideas into their own chapters, the glue that holds them together is diminished.

In the fall of 1942, Churchill felt he needed to pull everyone's attention back from the details to the big picture. That is the purpose of this chapter.

Of course, walking the trail in the mid-afternoon, everything is happening at the same time. It involves friction, knees, attitude, and the gear I am carrying. The walk may be painful or a breeze. Regardless, I like to put my mind into action and decide—whatever the circumstances—to Walk Well.

Each of the chapters of the book is meant to work with the others. In the preceeding chapter, I discussed many examples of ways I have found to lighten my pack. But, carrying a light pack helps me avoid blisters, too. Because my pack is light, I can wear shoes that are less likely to cause blisters. Inside the shoes, with a decreased weight on each foot, friction is decreased and blisters can more easily be avoided.

The light pack helps my knees, too. It keeps the muscles from tearing the tissues apart and allows me to walk great distances.

The bridging concept of my attitude and philosophy similarly impacts everything else on an afternoon's walk along the trail. Walking well involves enjoying the trail without much thought about a blister, or a chafed area, or my knees, or my pack. Walking well means being able to enjoy a sunny day, or a rainy day. It means being able to climb a 3000-foot mountain and come down the other side with a smile for my fellow hikers and a heart bursting with joy. Walking well means being at home in the woods. Walking well means knowing myself.

The whole idea of dealing with fear also transcends all the chapters. Walking well means walking free of fear, living in the woods. It is not visiting a foreign and hostile wilderness. Ridding myself of fear means applying prevention techniques that I know will work to keep blisters or chafing from popping up as problems. Replacing fear with innovation I am able to treat my knees in an improved way. In this new way, my knees will carry me great distances. Dealing with fear means taking everything out of my pack that is there as a result of fear.

The End of the Beginning 115

Footstomp: The last loose end is to drive deep the message of the book as a whole. In the military, there is a long tradition to footstomp important information. In classes where there will later be a test, the instructor obviously knows what will be on the test, and he wants to have everyone pass the test. So the instructor, from time to time will state a principle or fact and then stomp his foot. The message is clear. "What I just said will be on the test. Make sure y'all in the class remember it."

Mother Earth has a test in mind for many of us who would presume to walk and live in the forests. Here are the footstomps I think are worth remembering every day.

> *Blisters and chafing are caused by friction and moisture. There is no reason to keep going when early pain makes it clear that something needs to be changed. The best plan by far is to stop the formation of a blister or chafing sore before it becomes a major problem.*
>
> *Knee problems happen to hikers of all ages. Prevention of knee problems is possible with the healthy knee prescription.*
>
> *Losing the will to hike is a common problem. Its root cause can be stresses such as discouragement, lack of rest,*

weather, fear, or a physical problem. Having a personal plan for getting off the trail prevents a decision to stop a hike when it is dark, raining, and until the hiker has a chance to talk the decision over with a close friend or family.

While a lightweight pack is not the answer to everything, it does make everything easier. Getting pack weight down to a "Forget It" weight is important to feet, knees, and attitude. Since the goal is traveling by foot, being self-sufficient without carrying so much that it becomes a burden is crucial. The 15-pound pack turns backpacking into hiking.

Getting rest is critical, as is letting go of a number of fears. Carrying around a fear in my pack can be very heavy.

And finally, there is the whole notion of making the most of the opportunity. Hiking requires spending time away from the immediacy of obligations and the fellowship of family. Walking Well is a personal philosophy for walking to the end of a trail in the footsteps of the trail's pioneers. Walking Well is a way to live in the forest as a home. Walking Well is a good way to be remembered.

Index

A
alcohol stove 109
alone 60, 74, 76, 77, 99

B
baby powders 39
Big Four 109, 110
blister 11-17, 20, 21, 22, 26-30, 32, 71, 93, 114
Blisters 2, 4, 12, 13, 23
Bodyglide 21, 22, 39
boredom 78
bravery 92
Bryson 73

C
callus 14, 18, 26
canoe 93, 104
cartilage 46, 60
Chafing 2, 11, 30, 31
Clingman's Dome 3, 21, 93
Cold Spring 44
cotton 36, 37, 111

D
David Brill 74
Deep Gap 1, 4
Desitin 33
Duct tape 22

E
Earl Schaffer 26, 74, 90

F
Fear 108, 115, 116
fear 30, 73, 84, 88, 92, 105, 115-118
flute 21, 66, 107
forget it 102, 118

friction 12, 13, 15, 21-23, 27, 28, 32, 34, 36, 41, 75, 101
FugiBoots 57
fungus 39, 89

G
glucosamine 51, 59-61, 63
goals 83, 95
God 94
Grand UnificationTheory 99
groin 31, 35, 36, 39

H
hammock 65, 66, 70, 81, 84, 109
HeadsUp 1

I
ibuprofen 51, 58, 59

J
J.R. Tate 73
Jan D. Curran 73
Jardine 16, 19, 52, 83, 106

K
kilt 35, 40, 107
Kimsey Creek Trail 1
kitty litter 25
knee 4, 5, 17, 44-51, 54, 55, 58, 60-62, 67, 71, 93, 94

L
learning 4, 5, 73, 74, 90, 91, 97
Leki 57
loneliness 75, 77, 78, 92

N
nightmare 85, 86
NOC 44, 61

O
owl 66

P
pack 3, 16, 20, 32, 33, 48, 51, 52, 55, 63, 65, 66, 69, 70, 73, 82, 86, 87, 96, 101-111, 114-118
Patience (hiker) 58
perseverance 5, 92, 93
PUD 79

Q
quilt 66, 109

R
rain 15-18, 32, 69, 78, 80-82, 92, 96, 107, 110
Rainbow Springs 1, 11
rock garden 17

S
sandals 15, 17, 28, 29
sassafras (tree) 90
Sassafras Gap 48
Shane Steinkamp 69, 75, 98, 116
shear force 13, 14
shelter 2, 20, 31, 33, 44, 49, 65, 80, 83, 84, 88, 109
silnylon 20
socks 14, 17, 20, 22, 26, 28, 80, 107
Springer Mountain 3, 21, 86
Standing Indian 1, 2, 62
stress 48, 50, 51, 56, 75-78, 81, 82, 84, 89, 90-92, 95, 105
Sugar Loaf Gap 44, 49
sweat 12, 13, 15, 33-36
swimming trunks 37

T
talcum powder 38
tarp 70, 80, 81, 109
thru-hiker 1, 74

U
Udder Balm 39
ultralight 52, 73, 102, 105

V
Vandeventer 65
Vasque 19

W
Walk Well 7, 8, 10, 116
Wesser 14, 44, 61, 62
Winding Stair Gap 4

Z
Zaleski 53, 70

Ordering Information

* * *

If you can not find this book in your local outfitter you are welcome to order directly. Books are available at:

> http://www.wayahpress.com
> or
> orders@imrisk.com

* * *

Or you can use this handy form.

To: Wayah Press
      2566 Lantz Road
      Beavercreek, Ohio 45434

Please send me ___ copies of "A Wildly Successful 200-Mile Hike" @ 11.95 each.

I am enclosing _____

(Please add sales tax if appropriate (Ohio residents) and $2.50 for postage and handling. We can not ship to post office boxes or addresses outside the USA. Prices subject to change without notice.)

Ms./Mrs./Mr. _____
Address _____
City/State _____ Zip _____